D1413727

LEADERSHIP and
Dynamic Group Action

The Iowa State University Press

Ames, **Iowa, U.S.A.**

LEADERSHIP

and

Dynamic Group Action

**George M.
Beal**　　**Joe M.
Bohlen**　　**J. Neil
Raudabaugh**

ART BY HARRY WALSH

About the Authors

GEORGE M. BEAL has special interest in group processes, group formation and maintenance, social action, communication, and acceptance of ideas and practices. His publications include articles in the *Journal of Rural Sociology, Social Forces*, extension and research bulletins, *Public Opinion Quarterly*, the *Journal of Farm Economics* and the *Journal of Marketing*. He holds the doctor of philosophy degree from Iowa State University where he is professor of sociology.

JOE M. BOHLEN has a particular interest in farmer organizations and group processes, and in the diffusion of ideas — especially as it relates to farm practices. Together with Dr. Beal, he has conducted workshops and conferences across the country on how the principles of sociology and social psychology can be applied to everyday organizational problems. He holds the doctor of philosophy degree from Iowa State University where he is professor of rural sociology.

J. NEIL RAUDABAUGH pays special attention to group processes, diffusion of ideas, and leadership, especially as these relate to community development and group action. He has a master's degree from Iowa State University where he has done additional graduate study. He is assistant director of the Division of Extension Research and Training, Federal Extension Service, U.S. Department of Agriculture, Washington, D.C., and travels throughout the country assisting state extension personnel.

© 1962 The Iowa State University Press

All rights reserved. Printed in the U.S.A.

First paperback printing, 1967
Second paperback printing, 1969
Third paperback printing, 1971
Fourth paperback print.ng, 1972
Fifth paperback printing, 1973
Sixth paperback printing, 1974
Seventh paperback printing, 1975

First edition, 1962
Second printing, 1963
Third printing, 1965
Fourth printing, 1967

International Standard Book Number: 0–8138–0981–9

International Standard Book Number: 0–8138–0980–0

Library of Congress Catalog Card Number: 61–15797

Preface

THIS BOOK is for the millions of people who make up the myriad of groups operating within democratic societies — who are searching for ways to enhance the results of their group activities. Much of what is known about individual and group behavior has not been integrated and translated in meaningful terms so that it can be used by individuals in democratic groups to help them perform more efficiently and effectively.

Interpretations of the generalizations from Sociology and Social Psychology give further insight into human group behavior to those responsible people who are faced with the everyday problems of group living. Understanding these interpretations will help them be more efficient group members and leaders.

This book develops the logic of individual behavior in a group setting. The general framework of group behavior, which is the central theme of this book, provides the specific points which are elaborated upon. It already is a working tool of many group leaders and has proved that it helps develop more competent. group members and helps achieve group goals more effectively.

Group techniques to facilitate group action toward goals are not a bag of tricks into which leaders can reach when action is needed. Each technique has its own unique potentials. The chances for successful action are greatly enhanced if techniques are chosen on the basis of specific potentials, characteristics of the group, and the nature of the goal which is desired.

If this book strips group leadership of some of its beliefs about its divine powers and hereditary nature, it also should make leadership more realistic and more attainable to the group member who wishes to improve his human relations skills and assume greater responsibilities.

We have borrowed heavily from our professional colleagues. Because of our purposes in this book, we have not footnoted them except when we directly quote them. We have written this book to be used by the everyday man and woman rather than only by someone versed in special jargon of a scientific discipline.

If the reader finds this book to be an aid to becoming a more effective group member, the authors' purpose has been achieved.

GEORGE M. BEAL
JOE M. BOHLEN
J. NEIL RAUDABAUGH

Contents

8 CONTENTS

PART III

Evaluation

1. Group Interaction

Say! They're talking about **us!**

1.

Introduction

THE CONVENING OF GROUPS of persons to promote some sort of action or other is the great American pastime. *Fortune* magazine puts it like this:

> Except for a few intellectuals who don't believe in "joining," and the very, very poor who can't afford to, practically all adult Americans belong to some club or other, and most of them take part in some joint effort to do good. This prodigious army of volunteer citizens, who take time from their jobs and pleasure to work more or less unselfishly for the betterment of the community is unique in the world. It is, in a way, the mainspring as well as the safeguard of democracy. For whatever the silly rituals and absurdities of some of their organizations and the self interest of others, the volunteers are always ready to work and fight for what they think is right.[1]

---

[1] "The Busy, Busy, Citizen," *Fortune,* February 1951, p. 98.

That's us; no doubt of it! From our early days in school and on throughout life there is always an impending meeting. Most of us are a part of this "prodigious army of volunteer citizens." We may question and even resent, the time we take from "our jobs and pleasure" to work for community betterment, but we go right on doing it. This truly is the mainspring of democracy. We usually are ready to work and fight for what we think is right. Regrettably we sometimes fail to take time to learn what is right, and sometimes we fight harder with each other than we do for the "cause."

Often we doubt the wisdom of group action, especially when our groups make questionable decisions, dissolve in internal bickering, or fall under control of those who manipulate them for their own ends. But we also take time occasionally to marvel at how much we do accomplish; at how many important jobs do get done. It is a lasting satisfaction to take on a task for the common good and to see it through to completion, even though it may have been a routine chore. In retrospect we can remember many enjoyable experiences in our group activities. Perhaps we have felt ourselves grow in human relations skills as we have participated in these activities. Perhaps, as an even more rewarding experience, we have seen others grow under our leadership.

So it is to all of us, the members of the "prodigious army," that this book is directed. It should be of special value to those who are making their first tentative beginnings in community service and to young people who are still in school. It should prove useful to those professional and semiprofessional group leaders who are consciously trying to develop leadership in their groups. And finally it is directed toward any one of us who, as of today, has a special task to perform as president, officer, trustee, chairman, board member, councilman, or as a member of a committee or team.

Our interest may lie with the Red Cross, the P.T.A., the 4-H clubs, the Boy Scouts, or the Community Chest. Perhaps our allegiance is to the League of Women Voters or to a service club, garden club, or a little theater. Our group may operate in any one of a hundred areas: religious, political, civic, educational, trade, business, patriotic, fraternal, recreational, or just social. Even a listing of the virtually universal worthwhile groups would fill pages. And the word "worthwhile" is used advisedly, since it can never fail to impress an objective observer that the summation of all this helter-skelter group activity is to advance the common good. Usually this is because leadership develops within the group.

Most of us are leaders, have been leaders, or would like to become leaders. At least we would like to better understand the nature of the leash by which we are being led.

Many of us feel insecure within our groups. Perhaps we have had problems working with other group members. We should be willing to recognize that some of these problems revolve around ourselves as individuals. We may have difficulty communicating with others; when we speak we seem to "rub people the wrong way." We wonder what others really think of us and of the job we are doing.

Often we have difficulty figuring out what makes other group members "tick." Why don't certain members take more interest? What motivational force can be tapped

When we speak up we seem to "rub people the wrong way."

that will set Joe on fire? Why doesn't Mack speak up more often — his ideas are usually good. On the other hand, why does Hortense try to monopolize the discussion; how can we get her to see her proper role? Why do Maurice and Sylvia always disagree; do they really see things so differently, or is it a personality clash? Does Jack take part in the group activities only to enhance his prestige? These and a myriad of other questions rooted in human behavior inevitably arise.

Then there are the problems of the group as a whole. Do we really know what we are trying to accomplish; what our true goals are? Are they set up for long-range purposes, for this year, for this meeting, or for only a part of the meeting? Are there cliques within the group who see things differently? When there is general agreement on the objectives, then how do we differ on the proper means to accomplish these objectives? In the main are we interested only in pursuing our conventional methods and techniques? Is the group getting in a rut? Or does the group prefer to be in a rut and not strike out in new directions? Do the members really feel themselves a part of the group; do they feel responsible toward it?

Most of all, does anyone really take time to ask these questions; to evaluate our activities?

Again, how does our group relate to the outside? Do we really communicate with the rest of the community, or with the county, or state, or national organization of which we are a part? Do outsiders understand and appreciate what we are trying to do? Are we considered a snob organization, or a mutual admiration society? What are we doing to interpret ourselves to the rest of the world? Are we failing to achieve our ends because of this lack of external communication?

Such a question bee could be continued indefinitely. Any veteran committee worker could compile an equally formidable list. Many times it may seem that our own problem or the problem of our group is unique; probably this is rare. Problems tend to recur and to repeat themselves; they are the universal problems of human relations. One of the aims of this work is to analyze these problems, classify them, and provide basic understandings which may help in their solution.

What is an ideal board, committee, or council like? It might prove valuable to list some of the virtues of such a group so that we may compare it with our own.

The individual in this group feels secure, wanted, needed. He is able to accept his fellows and knows that they accept him. In such a group the interests and motivations of the members are readily tapped and rapid progress is made toward the goals selected. From time to time such progress is evaluated, as are the means by which it has been achieved. The group has a concept of leadership which does not put all the responsibility on a few persons. It tries to use rational methods of deciding on goals and the means of achieving them.

Unfortunately, few of us could apply this description in every detail to our own groups. Such smooth running perfection is seldom found in human institutions. More commonly we stagger, stutter, and clank toward our goal.

There are wide differences in the efficiency with which groups operate, ranging from near perfection to complete chaos. When effective action is obtained, we are not quite certain why things worked out so well. Actually, those who have led and have developed an efficiently working team have probably been "playing by ear." They have learned the hard way — largely by trial and error — which techniques work for them. They rarely can explain the reasons why a certain move was chosen or why it was successful. They have learned by experience that certain methods work, and often they are equally certain that other schemes will fail.

We say that these individuals have developed the "art" of leadership; that they can "feel" the temper of a group; that they seem to "sense" the right moves to make. Of course there is no such thing as a "natural born leader." Those who succeed so well are those who have consciously or subconsciously selected the proper methods from their experience. Unfortunately they often are unable to understand their own skill and are, therefore, incapable of conveying it to others. Also they often fail to adapt their methods to entirely new situations which may arise.

Even the most skilled leaders, as they try to develop group members around them into leaders, find it difficult to communicate the basic understanding of human behavior out of which skills emerge. However skilled they themselves may be, they often cannot transmit this skill to others.

The field of human relations is rapidly expanding beyond the confines of an art which is ruled by "common sense." One of the objectives of sociology is to bring scientific methods to bear on group behavior — analysis, experimentation, and valid generalization. From these studies are emerging certain concepts, principles, and tools which — when fully understood — will greatly enhance the achievement of leadership skill. Once understood, the basic principles of human relations can be applied skillfully and adequately without so much fumbling along under trial and error methods. Here, then, is the purpose of this book: the interpretation of those generalizations about human group behavior from sociology and social psychology in such a way as to make them applicable to the everyday problems of group living.

When the statement is made that people have within the range of their capabilities the ability to recognize, define, and solve their common problems, it is not assumed that any group has all the knowledge necessary. It is assumed that rational and intelligent people will seek out the necessary facts upon which to base a decision. A group taking action without having learned the facts is merely pooling the ignorance of its members and cannot hope for well-founded rational solutions.

Homans has stated the problem very aptly: "What the leader needs to have is not a set of rules, but a good method of analyzing the social situation in which he must act. If the analysis is adequate, a way of dealing with the situation will suggest itself."[2]

This might be compared to the statement that once a physician has diagnosed his patient's ailment the treatment should prove easy. However, this may be true only when the knowledge of the principles involved is basic and broad.

The ideas and generalizations just referred to so glibly are actually complex. For understanding, we use oversimplification.

It is hoped that the reader will expand, amplify, and better organize his more or less general ideas concerning the social psychology of the individual in the group, and of the group itself. It is further hoped that his awareness and understanding of the internal and external forces of group behavior (dynamics) can be so extended that he can put this knowledge to use in a practical way. To this end certain methods and techniques will also be described, always with the hope that the reader will be able to develop his own way of operation in order to fulfill his own needs and those of his group in varying situations.

---

[2] George C. Homans, *The Human Group*, Harcourt Brace, New York, 1950, p. 424.

Some leaders find it difficult if not impossible to communicate basic understandings.

Unless we are willing to cultivate the skills of group relationships, our democracy may go the way of the great democracies of history, and like the Athenians, we may destroy ourselves. In order to maintain our way of life, we must be eternally vigilant — not only toward external enemies, but toward ignorance, neglect, and lethargy within. There is a tendency today to think of democracy as something that is being stored for us somewhere in the great bureaucracy in Washington and to which we pay quadrennial lip service by voting in the presidential election.

Nothing could be farther from the truth. Democracy will live or die as a result of the day-to-day actions of all of us — when we attend or fail to attend the meeting — when we sign or refuse to sign the petition — when we accept or evade that committee appointment.

The fact that everyone in a democracy has the right to express his views carries with it the corollary fact that he has an equal responsibility to do so. Doing nothing is in itself often a most destructive act.

Our democratic American heritage can only be perpetuated by those who clearly see their rights, privileges, and responsibilities as exemplified by the democratic group. A hermit would waste his time reading this book; it is prepared for those who believe in democracy and who are willing to put some effort behind their belief.

2.

Democracy and the Democratic Group

EVERYONE PAYS LIP SERVICE to democracy. It has become a "status" word and anything which can attach itself to the word thereby attains status. Surely what the Russian Premier means when he alludes to a "democracy" is a far cry from what the President of the United States has in mind when he uses the same phrase. Each may sincerely believe that his is the only "true faith" and that his concept of democracy is the only valid one. Even within our own national culture there are many meanings of the word. Hence a definition of some length and detail is necessary.

THE TERM "DEMOCRACY"

The Greek root *Demos*, the people, is combined with the word *Kratos*, authority, to imply that all authority stems from the people. Under such a definition of democracy all who must abide by rules, regulations, and controls are entitled to a voice in their creation.

Democracy, then, is the means by which individuals are able to determine what they may ultimately expect in the way of freedom without impinging upon the rights of others. The degree of democracy achieved is not measured by the degree of such freedom to act, but by the extent to which those whose acts are thus abridged possess the authority to do the abridging.

It is right and proper that we should return to the founding fathers for the origins of our own democracy. Too frequently this means we believe that they presented it to us complete, with power steering and brakes, automatic turn signals, and electronic headlight dimmers. Not so. Our present concept of democracy is a product of many years of evolutionary growth. As a matter of fact it probably would horrify most of the founding fathers.

In general, these creators of our political system were obsessed with the idea of personal and political liberty and were not at all interested in democracy. Many of them were monarchists, or at least oligarchists, and our nation developed along those lines until the direction was changed by the one man who did have an abiding faith in democracy, Thomas Jefferson.

Jefferson recognized the evolving nature of democracy, the necessity for an ever broadening base, and the importance of universal education. He believed in the perfectability of man. But let us permit him to speak for himself; few have said these things better:

> Enlighten the people generally, and tyranny and oppressions of body and mind will vanish like evil spirits at the dawn of the day.[3]

> I know no safe depository of the ultimate powers of the society but the people themselves; and if we think them not enlightened enough to exercise their control with a wholesome discretion, then the remedy is not to take it from them, but to inform their discretion.[4]

---

[3] Letter to P. S. DuPont de Nemours. April 24, 1816.
[4] Letter to William Charles Jarvis. Sept. 28, 1820.

To better appreciate the expanding concept of democracy it is worthwhile to examine the context in which the founding fathers spoke when they referred to "the people" or to "the electorate." We have become accustomed to thinking of the beginnings of our democracy in the New England town meeting, or in the deliberative bodies of the various colonies. We seldom remember that these groups were made up of "the people" only as they were freemen as opposed to slaves, only if they were not indentured or apprenticed, only if they could read and write, and only if they owned real property. Most of all, no recognition as citizens was accorded women!

Even Jefferson, with all his insight, idealism, and faith in the future, was unable to project his ideas nearly so far as we have come. He did not believe that man would ever become truly responsible in his behavior unless he owned property. When he made the Louisiana Purchase this was uppermost in his mind, for he foresaw a vast nation of small landholders. Even his advanced thinking failed to visualize the day when ownership of an automobile or of common stocks would serve the same purpose. He surely did not envisage the possibility that vested rights such as pension security or collective bargaining would do the same thing.

We have discussed chiefly the political aspects of democracy, since the origins of the term are in our political past. As democracy has grown and expanded it has become more and more apparent that this concept invades

Even in our own country democracy is defined in many ways.

every aspect of our lives, not only in our political thinking but in the way we carry out all our joint ventures.

Free men everywhere work hard to maintain their common institutions: their churches, schools, businesses, and governments. Many of the most important activities relevant to solving common problems take place at the community level — often by means of the social structure which we call the *formal democratic group*. The essence of democracy may be observed in these groups — small entities composed of people who interact in an atmosphere of tolerance and respect. It is a part of the American dream that by the devotion of time and energy the group can solve problems and satisfy needs with which the solitary individual could not hope to cope.

This penchant of the American people was first documented in the early 1800's when Alexis de Tocqueville, that astute observer of American life, wrote:

> A citizen may conceive of some need which is not being met. What does he do? He goes across the street and discusses it with his neighbor. Then what happens? A committee comes into existence, and then the committee begins functioning on behalf of their need, and you won't believe this, but it's true . . . all of this is done without reference to any bureaucrat. All of this is done by the private citizens on their own initiative.[5]

If then, we have somehow approached the true meaning of democracy, and if it is best implemented by the formal democratic group, then how may this group be described?

It is the voluntary association of a group of equals into an entity capable of action — and recognized as such by both members and nonmembers. Further, it is a social structure within which the members partake of a pattern

---

[5] Alexis de Tocqueville, *Democracy in America*, New American Library, New York, 1950.

of interaction based on the premise that each individual has both the right and the responsibility to contribute to its tasks.

Such a definition, by its nature very broad, only begins to describe the formal democratic group. Usually such an organization has a name; often there is a constitution and set of bylaws. Elected officers are the general rule, regularly scheduled meetings are held, and a wide variety of activities are carried out. There are literally thousands of such groups and many examples come readily to mind.

THE GROUP PROCESS

The fundamental belief of our American democracy is in the dignity of man. As a result of such belief we have devised the group process as a means of governing our affairs. In every phase of living we find people working in groups to solve their problems.

The church board is an example. So is the township farm extension group and the board of the union local. The local chapter of the Federated Women's Clubs and the committee for Little League teams all operate as formal democratic groups. One could as well name the board of directors of the most gigantic corporation, or the powerful finance committee of the United States Senate. All of our governmental units down to the smallest locally appointed board function along the same line.

Such groups are not unknown in other democracies, but Americans are most unusual in their faith in the formal democratic group as a means for solving problems. Even in far-advanced democracies the "people" have delegated policy making as well as the day-to-day activities to the rich, the wellborn, or to "the establishment." In other countries small oligarchies or even dictatorships control the affairs of men. But in America we continue to have faith that the people, when they have access to the facts, can make better decisions than others can make for them.

Because of these faiths and beliefs, our lives are constantly surrounded by the group process in action, and constant claims on our time and interest are being made by this myriad of groups.

It is the authors' opinion that the following assumptions are fundamental to a faith in the democratic group process:

1. Groups of ordinary people have, within the range of their capacities, the ability to recognize, define, and solve their common problems and to satisfy their common needs by working together.

2. Group action is based upon group consensus achieved through the participation of all members according to their differential abilities to contribute. It follows from this that group activities are more acceptable and more successful when evolved by the group as a whole than when a product of the drive of any individual or clique. It is a corollary that all group members, not only certain leaders, are responsible for the quality of group production.

3. Group productivity can be increased through efforts both of the entire membership and of individual members to improve their human relations skills, to foster better group interaction, and also by continual evaluation of progress toward goals and of the means used to attain such progress.

The essential characteristic of the democratic group is that decisions are made by the group as a whole with each member participating on the basis of his skills and interests. Ideally, a further characteristic is that ideas are evaluated on the basis of merit and relevance to goal attainment rather than on the status of their proponents.

Furthermore, a group is a social unit whose process can be analyzed. The functioning of a group is under the control of its members and it can become more efficient and more effective; in a word, it can mature. The first step in such a program of improvement is analysis of the participation and interaction of the members. The formal democratic group is neither a laissez-faire nor an autocratic group. The laissez-faire (let alone) group is characterized by its lack of organization. A good example may be the ordinary precinct organization of a political party. The leadership tends to be passive and the influence of the membership on each other is casual. Only as an election approaches does the group show any signs of life. Usually a caucus is held — a most desultory organization meeting.

The great defect of such a group is its inability to accomplish any purpose. Individual initiative is stifled and progress is usually nil. When accomplishments are made it is because a more definitive organization begins to take place — usually when a "hot" election shapes up. At this time the group often becomes truly democratic and real progress is made.

Unfortunately an even greater defect of the laissez-faire group may appear. It is easy for individuals to seize control of such a group for their own ends and convert it into an autocracy. This is what happens when machine politics takes over. Some of our most venal political situations occur because of lack of organization of local groups.

The autocratic group is under the domination of an individual or a "power clique." The rank and file members may go through the motions of democratic behavior, but they are present only to "rubber stamp" the decisions of the leadership. In groups of this type (and they are very common) there are wide status differences between the members and communication tends to be one-way — from the leaders to the followers. Ideas are accepted on the basis of their origin, not on their intrinsic merit. When the leader (on a basis of prestige or power seizure) advances a proposal it is usually accepted. When a member attempts to reverse the direction of communication he is usually "squelched."

The classic example of the autocratic group is the military unit. Another good example is found in certain small businesses which have a board of directors elected from the stockholders. Often a single individual or a clique owns the controlling interest and the board, made up of minority stockholders, merely echoes the program, wants, and desires of the control group. The autocratic group usually carries the seeds of its own destruction. Removal, illness, or death of the autocratic leader normally results in a contest for power among his successors. Such a "palace revolution" may result in another dictator or a clique seizing power. It may result in the formation of a democratic group, or the group may dissolve into oblivion.

Evaluations of the relative effectiveness of the three major types of group process (democracy, autocracy, and laissez faire), have been carried out in many ways and at many levels. Of special note are some which have involved boys' clubs, industrial groups, educational groups, and some experimental groups created solely for this purpose. The results are uniform enough that certain generalizations seem to be warranted.

Democratic groups have greater motivation toward work, more member satisfaction, and greater productivity. There is less discontent among members and less evidence of frustration and aggression. There is more friendliness, cooperation, and group-centered *esprit* when democracy prevails. Despite the group orientation it has been demonstrated that more individual initiative is displayed. When a group or its action is criticized there is little or no tendency to use an individual as a scapegoat.

The autocratic group cannot compete with the democratic in all-round productivity. Within these groups are found excessive irritability, hostility, and aggression, often directed toward fellow members as well as toward the autocratic leader. The members of such a group are apt to be apathetic in their general attitude even when secretly discontented. Individuals are much more dependent and show a minimum of creativity. When the autocrat is absent little or no action ensues. Criticism of fellow members or attempts to dominate them are much more prevalent in this setting than when democracy prevails.

The principle characteristic of the laissez-faire group is its lack of productivity. Individuality is often exhibited, but cannot be channeled into useful fields. The general feeling of lack of progress tends to make the membership uninterested and apathetic.

A basic principle of rational behavior is that the means used must be consistent with the ends sought. This principle applies to both individual and group behavior. Thus, if one of the ends of our society and the groups that operate within it is to promote the basic goals of democracy, it would seem logical that democratic, rather than authoritarian or laissez-faire means should be used to attain those goals. Both the logic of the use of democratic means in a democratic society and the research findings reported in the discussion above point to the importance of using democratic group procedures for effective goal accomplishment.

Every group assembled does not necessarily have within it all of the needed information and resources to make valid decisions. When a group proceeds to make decisions and

ctions without considering all of the relevant informa-
available from expert sources it probably is acting on
he basis of "pooled ignorance." Groups appear to be as
guilty as individuals acting as separate entities of not seeking relevant expert information before making decisions.

It should be emphasized that for all purposes the group
has not *always* been shown to be superior to the individual,
nor has the democratic group always been shown to be
superior to the more centrally directed type. Especially
where certain limited objectives are concerned there may
be advantages in nondemocratic action. In the long run,
however, and whenever there are situations of great complexity, groups arrive at a larger proportion of correct solutions than do individuals or groups dominated by an individual.

In industry, among housewives, in the classroom, and
even in the military it has been demonstrated that the involvement of people in group discussion and the reaching
of decisions in a democratic atmosphere leads to more favorable attitudes toward the decision and better compliance
with it.

One industrial study indicated that participation in decision making by all members of the group resulted in
greater productivity, less resistance to change, and a lower
turnover rate of employment than did either committee
decision making or careful explanation of decisions made
by others. Another study points out that when supervisors
and subordinates were involved to a high degree in research

. . . the group did not use an individual
member as a scapegoat.

planning and in the interpretation and analysis of the findings the results were better understood, emotionally accepted, and utilized.

During World War II a campaign was waged to induce housewives to use some of the less popular cuts of meat such as heart, kidney, and sweetbreads. With some groups the lecture method was used; with others a short opening statement followed by a group discussion was concluded by a show of hands by those willing to try these meats. The second method was *ten times* more effective than the first.

Similar results were obtained in a study which aimed at increasing the use of milk in the home; the group discussion method was more effective by a ratio of 3 to 1. In this experiment the duration of the results was also checked and found to be greatly increased following discussion group methods.

When individuals commit themselves to act in a certain way their decision is strengthened by an awareness that others are similarly committed. They do not wish to lose status by failure to follow through on a decision witnessed by their peers. One of the strongest motivating forces for an individual is to be respected and to have status in the eyes of the members of groups to which he considers it important to belong. This principle is one of the most important in establishing the superiority of group action over individual action.

It is obvious from the above discussion that human beings participate in many kinds of group situations in their efforts to satisfy their needs and desires and that these groups have influence in the lives of these individuals. In this book our major interest is, however, in the formal democratic group, and its major characteristics may be listed as follows:

1. The goals and objectives of such a group are established by group interaction.

2. The means adopted to achieve these are determined by the same process.
3. The interaction process is such that each member feels both freedom to contribute and responsibility for success.
4. Group consensus prevails, even though individuals do not completely agree, but disagreeing individuals feel free to present their points of view.
5. Ideas are dealt with on a basis of their value to the group rather than on a basis of who introduces them.
6. Those in position of formal leadership recognize that their major role is that of facilitating group process.

3.

Leadership in the Democratic Group

IT IS PROBABLE that without leadership no group can produce worthwhile action in the direction of its goals. But what is *leadership*? This word, like democracy, means many things to many people.

Just as our concept of democracy is a growing and expanding one, so is there a parallel growth and development of the meaning of leadership. The expansion of the democratic principle has demanded that new types of leadership arise.

It is easy to credit a leader with both the successes and failures of a group. Perhaps the true virtues, or faults, were those of the group itself. Many believe that the leader casts his personality over the group, but more frequently the opposite situation occurs. Much of this vagueness arises from the looseness of the meaning of the term *leader* in the English language. It is used to designate both one who commands and one who guides. In actual practice these may be as widely at variance as the chairman of the P.T.A. meeting and a Marine platoon leader in combat. Yet both are leaders.

The myth of the "born leader" is one common idea of the past which will not stand up under modern research. It was no doubt perpetuated by those with hereditary authority and was given support by the frequency with which sons succeeded fathers as leaders. One must remember that these sons were given training in leadership almost from birth. It was no accident that Aristotle went from Athens to Macedon to instruct the young Alexander. It was planned that way. In the early days of our culture, leadership was of necessity confined to the few, since knowledge and freedom from superstition were only available to a few.

Frazer, in *The Golden Bough,* states that the rise of despotic leaders was a necessary concomitant to emergence from savagery, since in primitive societies there was no mechanism by which large numbers of persons could become simultaneously enlightened. Hence history is replete with stories of the military leader who seized power and subsequently effected great civil and economic reforms. So the "great man" theory of history arose, culminating in the eulogies of Carlyle in the nineteenth century. Only more recently have historians begun to question this concept and to consider whether leaders might have automatically arisen in response to forces at play too complex for man to control. Even Toynbee — popular protagonist for the interplay-of-forces idea of history — concedes Frazer's point that leaders must arise, and at least in the emergence from savagery to civilization they must be despotic.

Many great leaders of the past were military leaders. The military leader functions in a predetermined organization so complete that all the duties and responsibilities of each level of leadership are spelled out in advance. The "chain of command" is inviolate, and within such a framework an individual with very few qualities of leadership may function efficiently and even effectively. This is the entire basis of the bureaucratic organization. Many organizations follow this pattern, though the military one is the most characteristic. The leader of such a group has been very aptly termed the *bureaucratic leader.* In our modern organizations, particularly governmental, he often seems to be the indispensable man, even when ostensibly and basically other philosophies of leadership should prevail.

Another type has been termed the *passive leader.* He has developed a following because he happens to possess certain talents, skills, or traits which are much admired, not by any deliberate effort toward leadership on his part. Contemporary examples of such leadership might include Mickey Mantle in sports or Pablo Picasso in the world of art.

The leader who achieves his role almost entirely through personal magnetism has attracted the most interest in the writing of the past and still dominates some of the most fascinating chapters in history. He has been called the *personal power* or *charismatic* leader. All the great religions were founded by leaders of this ilk and many political leaders have possessed the same ability. Most dictators begin as this kind of leader, though it soon becomes necessary for them to solidify their power by developing a bureaucracy. They are followed because of their original attractiveness or "charisma" and most of their followers soon become convinced that such leadership will maximize the ends which they seek.

DEMOCRATIC LEADERSHIP

In a group of equals working together to solve a mutual problem, another type of leadership will emerge. Ideally, and most commonly in actual practice, this will be *democratic leadership.*

The democratic leader evolves out of the group of which he is a part, rather than by creating a following of his own. There are inevitably those whose ideas influence the others more than theirs are in turn influenced *by* others. In such a group a tradition builds up that certain individuals are the most capable for certain tasks. When a crisis arises the membership turns to these individuals more readily than to untried personnel. These members are leaders, and they are democratic leaders.

In general, a leader of a democratic group is one who epitomizes the values and norms of his group. The group considers that his judgment is most in line with that of the membership, that the alternatives which he proposes fit in with the value system of the group. Often it may be said that he usually puts the well-being of the group ahead of his own desires where they conflict.

The democratic leader has the ability to perceive the direction in which the group is moving and to move in that direction more rapidly than the group as a whole. His foresight into the means and ends which will help the group is superior and for this reason he is chosen, or becomes a leader.

Democracy moves slowly. One of the reasons for this is that a democratic leader is seldom one who is far superior to his group. Groups which form tend originally to be made up of peers, or equals. If such a group happens to consist largely of average citizens, it is unlikely that they will select a member who has far superior qualifications as their leader. They will select one who is somewhat ahead of them in qualifications, but if the gap is too great they fail to communicate and thus fail to make use of this leadership material which exists within their group. In our general culture the distrust of one of superior ability is anti-intellectualism, and it pervades all levels of group behavior. This tendency has made some persons impatient with democracy, but as expressed in the previous chapter, the alternatives are worse in the long run. Someone has expressed the problem like this: "In a democracy the ideal solution to a problem is almost never achieved, but some solution is eventually reached, and it is a solution with which everyone can live."

Pure types of leadership seldom exist. An historical anecdote may help to point up this fact. In the summer of 1832 there was a minor Indian uprising along the Mississippi known as the Black Hawk War. As was customary at the time a company of volunteers was raised and according to the custom of those more democratic days they held an election and chose their captain. Thus the young man selected was obviously a democratic leader, but by virtue of the military organization now became a bureaucratic leader. The interesting speculation is whether or not the soldiers of that company really recognized the personal magnetism of the man who was to become one of the greatest "charismatic" leaders in American history, Abraham Lincoln.

Up to this point the personalized term *leader* and the abstraction *leadership* have been more or less intermingled without regard to certain subtle differences. Paul Pigors, in his book *Leadership or Domination,* says: "Leadership is a process of mutual stimulation, which by successful interplay of relevant individual differences, controls human energy in pursuit of a common cause." If this is a logical definition, then a leader is anyone whose ideas are helping to give direction toward the common goals of the group. Or to paraphrase once more: *An individual is a leader in any social situation in which his ideas and actions influence the thoughts and behavior of others.*

It may readily be seen that acceptance of this concept de-emphasizes the leader and emphasizes leadership. And

An individual is a leader when his ideas or actions influence others.

in the highest development of the democratic group leadership is not concentrated, but is diffused throughout the membership. The greater the degree of this diffusion, the more effectively democratic is the group.

Such a view of leadership has little to do with the formally elected leaders of the small democratic group, the chairmen, presidents, and other officers. In a group of this kind these officers recognize that their formal leadership is situational and that other group members may perform functions equal to or superior to their own.

If leadership is, as we have said, the process of influencing people by ideas, then there is no limit to the number of leaders that can function within a group. In fact the more the better because the very act of leadership, in whatever form observed, develops initiative, creativity, and mature responsibility.

Furthermore, leadership of this kind is not a mystic something or other that one individual has and another has not. It is learned behavior and anyone can improve himself in it by proper study and application. Such leadership is also situational and in the ideal group will shift from person to person depending upon the task at hand.

In a truly democratic group, leadership is diffused. Every member is a leader whenever he contributes an idea that is needed at a particular time. Leadership passes from person to person as each member contributes something needed in the process of achieving group goals.

It has been stated that the democratic group succeeds on the assumption that people, given the necessary facts, can make better decisions than others can make for them. One of the weaknesses of group democratic action is embodied in the phrase "if given the facts." All too often decisions are made emotionally, on a basis of ignorance. This raises another point. Since every member of a democratic group is a leader or a potential leader it becomes his duty to inform himself regarding the problems of that group. If he is to make intelligent decisions and suggestions for action which will provide leadership for his group he must accept responsibility. Responsibility calls for knowledge: knowledge of the group and its goals, knowledge of alternate means by which the goals may be sought, and general knowledge of the area in which the group operates. Thus we come full circle in pointing up the relationship between democracy and education.

Proper answers must often be sought beyond the group — from experts and resource people. Willingness to seek outside information is often a true mark of maturity in either an individual or a group. The anti-intellectual approach tends to belittle special knowledge and ability, to the loss of everyone.

Democracy is vitally important in American life. Many of the decisions which culminate in national policy begin at the "grass roots," where ideas tend to originate. If we are to have maximum benefits from this fact every individual should have some insight into the processes of leadership. He should recognize the great importance of having every group member feel himself a leader, or at least a potential leader, with a willingness to accept the responsibilities this entails.

4.

A Framework for the Study of Group Action

It is important to establish a framework upon which may be draped the many diverse ideas regarding group formation, group action, group goals, and group methods. These ideas are not simple, and it is necessary to distill, refine and organize them in such a manner that the reader can marshall them wisely into an appreciation of the principles of human relations inherent in group behavior. The group leader looking for a "bag of tricks" or a set of rules to apply to all situations will be disappointed. Analytical diagnosis of the social situation must always come before application.

Let us begin with an oversimplification. All forms of life have requirements for existence which they try to satisfy. Man differs in that he is a telic being; he can project his thoughts and desires into the future. He is thus motivated and acts with regard to certain objectives. Through his thinking process he sets up goals toward which he strives, and his actions have meaning only in relation to such objectives.

To state this another way: Since man alone is able to think, he alone selects goals which represent desires as well as needs. Having desired, and having established goals, he proceeds to act in such a way as he thinks will enable him to reach these goals.

The same basic analysis can be applied to groups, since they are made up of individuals. Groups also have desires and act to satisfy them. To attain their goals they must employ certain means.

Here then is the most elementary breakdown of the group process: Groups, like individuals, develop wants and desires, some of which they establish as goals. In their effort to achieve those goals they select certain techniques. These are the three basic elements in the group process: the group, the goals, and the techniques.

Simplified pictures of complicated subjects should never be taken completely literally. The comparison just drawn between individual and group behavior is a case in point. The individual, within his own mental capabilities and background, chooses his goals and adopts his means largely of his own volition, even though this is modified by the social groups in which he moves or would like to move. Group choices, either of goals or of means, are a product of the interaction of many forces within the individual members, between the individual members, and in response to external pressures. Thus the individual choice may represent a fairly simple, straightforward, action and reaction. Any action on the part of a group represents a resolution of numerous forces which must in some way be directed.

Too often we ask for "a bag of tricks."

THE GROUP

This can be illustrated schematically by a circle, which represents the *group* (Figure 4.1). To further simplify the problem, it will be assumed that the group already exists and that certain motivations are at work. The small figures within the circle represent the *individual members*. The arrows, large and small, represent various forces at work.

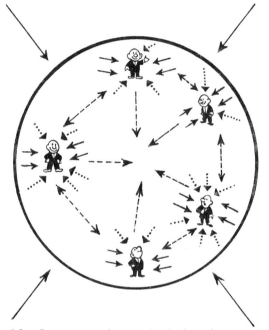

Fig. 4.1 — Forces at work on individuals within a group.

The individual member is unique in that he is different from every other member. He brings to the group certain general and specific interests, drives, and motivations. He has certain expectations and aspirations which he may or may not have translated into goals. He brings with him definite values, attitudes, habits, feelings, and beliefs. These things, which have applied largely to himself, he now also applies to the group members and to the group as a whole.

These basic individual drives are indicated by the small arrows beside each figure.

While all the above-listed individual traits might be referred to as positive forces, it must be remembered that the individual also brings to the group certain negative forces. He is a human being with premonitions, frustrations, inhibitions, and fears. He has developed certain adjustment patterns to his past failures. He introduces these patterns into the group, as illustrated by the small dotted arrows about the individual figure. There are other negative traits. Perhaps the member is not really interested in the group or its goals but brings an ulterior motive, a "hidden agenda" such as personal gains. He may have a self image of the role he would like to play in the group. This may be a totally different role than that for which he is fitted.

In the process of interaction within the group, certain new forces arise — forces which originate in the individual, it is true, but occur only because of his interaction with the other members.

These *lines of force* which arise out of group relationships are illustrated by the arrows with long, broken shafts. Notice that they join each member with every other member, and also each member to the group as a whole. An individual reacts not only to other individuals in the group but also to the fact that he is a member of the group.

It is difficult to express these forces in familiar terms. Authors speak of the atmosphere or climate of a group, of communication patterns, of "we-feelings," of general role definition, of group standards, and of human relation skills, to name only a few. For present purposes it will probably suffice to speak of lines of force generated within the individual, and lines of force generated as a result of individuals reacting with each other and with the group as a whole. Together, they are commonly called the *internal dynamics* of group behavior.

Further energies exert themselves on the group. No group operates in a vacuum and the norms of the culture of which the group is a part exercise a constant pressure from

. . . others are not acceptable.

without. This is illustrated by the solid arrows, and their summation makes up the external dynamics of the group. Every group feels the force of the community or societal value system of which it is a part; it will probably take up and carry out certain actions which are "acceptable" and reject others which are not acceptable.

As one example of external forces which impinge upon the group, every group has other groups to which it "refers" to determine what its actions should be, or how acceptable its past actions have been. These may be called "reference groups" and may be subdivided into two types, normative and comparative.

Normative reference groups have expectation patterns (norms) together with some ability to enforce these norms on others. A typical normative reference group is the "community" which expects each group to perform certain functions for certain purposes and for certain people. Through social pressure, the giving of recognition and "status," the community has the power to more or less enforce these expectations. The "parent" organization of any local group (for example the state organization of the P.T.A.) is also a normative reference group and demands certain performance from its affiliated local groups.

Comparative reference groups are groups with which other groups compare themselves. Possibly they are groups which it seems desirable to imitate, or groups whose errors it would seem desirable to avoid. These reference groups influence the membership, objectives, and activities of other groups and help to set the prestige rating of the group in the community. These are only some of the external forces which prod, impede, or maintain status quo in groups and which will be discussed in more detail in Chapter 7.

GROUP GOALS

Why does a group exist? It must have objectives — ends which it seeks — whether these are explicitly stated or only implied. Sometimes groups seem to have little conception of the reasons for their existence, what they are trying to accomplish, or why they take part in the activities in which they do. They exist largely because "they always have" and people continue to hold meetings. But many groups have, on the contrary, more specific purposes. Often they are well defined and integrated. Such objectives may be long range as well as shore range — they may be single- or multiple-purpose objectives, and they may be specific or general.

If a group is to be productive it must have goals and they must be understood. If a group is to make progress, goals must exist against which such progress can be measured. If effective means are to be chosen, progress toward goals is the only way by which their effectiveness can be measured. Adequate objectives are a prime requisite of effective group action. Whence do they come? In a democratic group situation such as we have been discussing they are chosen. And who chooses them? The group itself, under the stimulus of the forces already described, which we have called dynamics, internal and external.

We proceed with our diagram by producing another circle, this time in the shape of a target entitled *goals* (Figure 4.2).

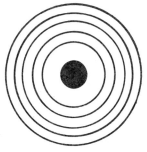

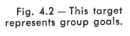
Fig. 4.2 — This target represents group goals.

TECHNIQUES

A third portion of the framework is illustrated by a square (Figure 4.3). This represents the means by which the wants and desires of the group are translated into goals and also the means by which these goals are sought and gained, and is entitled *techniques.*

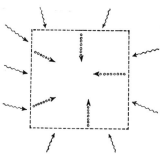

Fig. 4.3 — This diagram represents the techniques used to reach group goals.

A *group technique,* a predesigned pattern for human interaction, offers a better potential for progress toward goals than does unstructured random behavior. Many techniques are available. Some are quite standardized and traditional, while others are of a more spontaneous nature. In addition to an understanding of the nature of the group and its goals, one also should know the potentials and limitations of the available techniques. This will be discussed at length later.

A proper technique has the potential for activating individual drives and motivations and for stimulating both internal and external dynamics so that the forces may be better integrated and directed toward the goals of the group. This assumes that the proper technique has been chosen and that it is applied in the proper social setting.

The arrows within the square represent the potential driving forces of various methods which, in the abstract, may be thought of in familiar terms such as informality, spontaneity, control, and diffusion of responsibility. Some of these represent negative potentials, such as nondirected participation, excessive emotional involvement, lack of control, or inadequate personnel. It will be noted that we have made liberal use of the word "potential." This is in recognition of the fact that no technique, formal or informal, enters into the dynamics of group action *until it is applied*. Only when in actual use do the potential forces inherent in a technique become real forces, and only then can they enter into the dynamics of the situation.

The arrows outside the square represent the characteristics of the milieu in which the group operates, insofar as they will have an influence over the types of technique used. These characteristics may vary widely from one group to another, and even at different times with the same group. It is easy to see that a technique which was applicable at one time might not be at another because of the climate in which the group was operating. Similarly, comparable groups operating in different surroundings might find methods which were excellent for one situation to be entirely inappropriate for another.

Usually the more traditional techniques by which group action is stimulated are referred to by formal names. Some of the more familiar are discussion, panel, symposium, role-playing, dialogue, interview, and committee hearing. We may be sure that there is always some technique at work

We can all be socially creative.

within a group. It may be at a subconscious level, but is nevertheless operative. Man, by his very nature, is always working toward a goal and employing means for achieving it, whether he is aware of it or not. Even doing nothing may be a technique — since it may cause others to react.

In Part II there will be an extensive discussion of formal group techniques. It is the real hope, however, that interest will be directed toward *devising* new techniques; toward social creativeness.

We can all be socially creative! Certain basic understandings of human relations skills are needed. Along with these the possession of the principles of group behavior and the tools of analysis will lead to ways of dealing with each situation. Such creativity will inevitably lead to greater group productivity and many personal and common satisfactions.

THE COMPLETE FRAMEWORK

We can now combine the three figures — the *group*, the *goals*, and *techniques* — into one, using algebraic symbols (Fig. 4.4). The group, plus the techniques, equals the goals.

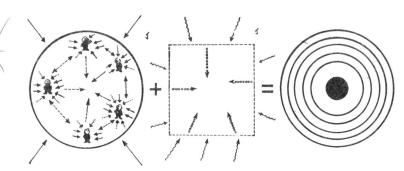

Fig. 4.4 — The group, plus the techniques, equals the goals.

At first glance it may seem that a static system has been set up, that the elements of group behavior have been broken down into three separate parts and that we can discuss them separately. Only in the most elementary sense is this true. Individuals and groups change; only they can select their goals and determine the means by which to seek them. The group process is an ever-changing thing and the parts of its structure are separated only for ease in study, never for subdivision.

Permeating the whole structure which has been developed is man's value system — what he considers important. Values are the guides by which individuals and groups determine their goals. Man's interests and motivations come from this value system, which organizes his experience and orients his past. Values will determine what individuals come together to form a group, how they will interact, and how they will select their goals and adopt their techniques. The individual in the group setting thus becomes the next focal point of attention.

CHAPTER

5.

The Individual in a
Group Setting

WHY ARE WE HERE at all? Why do people join groups and participate in their activities? Probably nearly everyone has asked himself these questions as he has looked about a meeting room. Again, why do people react so differently to the various ideas and situations which confront the group? These questions are basic, and might be summed up as: Why do people behave the way they do?

To answer this in breadth and depth would obviously carry us beyond the scope of this book. A limited discussion aimed at locating the individual member within the group must suffice.

MAN, THE THINKING, ORGANIZING BEING

Man differs in one great quality from the lower animals. The elemental drives for food, shelter, and sexual gratification are present in man, as in any animal; but because man can think abstractly his desires go infinitely further. What is this ability to think abstractly?

Fundamentally it is the ability to recall mental images of past experiences, to make value judgments about them, and to project the lessons of such judgments into the future. Using this ability man can benefit by his experience and by the experience of his fellow men, living and dead, through communication systems. Symbols, words, and gestures have been developed to communicate phenomena which are part of the general experience of mankind, not necessarily a part of his personal sensory experience. The following simple illustration may sharpen this aspect of the differences between animal and man.

A mother bear, in order to train her cubs, might take them with her as she tears apart bee trees and eats honey. The cubs observe and do likewise. Thus they are conditioned to smell honey and find it. If the air is suddenly filled with the odors of man, steel, and gunpowder, the mother bear can take off full speed in the opposite direction and the cubs will follow. This conditions them to the fact that man-smell means "run away."

This is simple imitation. A mother bear cannot sit back in the quiet and safety of the den and communicate to her cubs that certain insects of the order Hymenoptera gather nectar and, through a special digestive process, deposit this product in waxen containers inside hollow trees. She cannot

Why are we here at all?

tell them that this honey has a unique odor and that the trees may also be located by following the bees. They must be beside her as she does these things in order to go through the direct sensory experience. She cannot tell them about man and guns; she can only run away and have the cubs do the same.

On the other hand, man — using word symbols derived from the thinking process — can tell his fellow men about these experiences without ever having to take them to the actual situations.

With this ability to think abstractly, man projects himself into the future. He establishes goals toward which he can direct his actions and he anticipates problems which will contront him. Also, because of this ability, he is able to have a mental picture of himself as a social being. He visualizes himself as a person associating with others more or less like himself. He has ideas of how others regard him and what they expect of him. He has ideas about whether or not he is liked by others and whether or not others consider him to be important to them and their lives. He evaluates others and he often acts on the basis of how he thinks others are evaluating him. He can consider these evaluations and expectations of his fellow men in terms of their potentialities for enhancing or impeding the attainment of goals which he desires.

Only man, because of this ability to think about abstractions, can project himself into the future and establish in his mind the things he wants in his future. He can communicate his complex thoughts to others and in turn receive similar communication from them.

A dog can be conditioned to come for food at the sound of a whistle simply by providing him with rations every time his master whistles in a certain way. A bear cub learns to avoid man by associating the odor of man and the mother bear running away. These constitute a simple stimulus-response reflex arc. Given a stimulus — the

. . . every time one whistles in a certain way.

whistle — the dog responds by coming to the master to receive the food or other rewards. The bear cub is nudged along by the mother bear or cuffed behind the ear. A system of rewards and punishments is built around immediate sensory experience and acceptable response. Nonacceptable response leads to hungry dogs and dead bears.

Man, because he has this ability to deal with abstractions, responds to many stimuli in different ways. Man not only *can* think in abstractions, but he *must* think this way. His responses are always based upon his *interpretations* of the stimuli which he receives. Interpretation of stimuli include: (1) recall of similar stimuli received in the past; (2) responses made to these similar stimuli; (3) comparison of the existing circumstances surrounding the immediate stimulus to which he anticipates responding with the conditions surrounding the response patterns of the past experiences; (4) evaluations of the relative satisfactions received from the ways in which he responded in the past; and (5) an evaluation and comparison of the goals and ends which he desired when he responded to former stimuli with the goals or ends which he hopes to achieve in responding to the present stimulus.

It is only after an individual has gone through these thought processes that he responds to the stimulus. There are great differences in the degree to which various individuals go through these steps.

When an individual receives a stimulus which is familiar to him because of the number or intensity of previous similiar experiences, he remembers these past experiences, what responses he made, and how satisfied he was with the results of his subsequent behavior. For the average American, an alarm clock's ringing demands very little considered thought as to the nature of the response because it is a stimulus which has been received many times before. However, this same average American might respond quite differently to the sound of a lute playing because he probably has not received this stimulus before.

After an individual has recalled similar stimuli and his responses to them, he considers his past responses in the light of his satisfactions with the outcomes. He considers the circumstances under which those past stimuli were received and compares them with the conditions surrounding the immediate stimulus to which he must respond. The conditions surrounding a given stimulus greatly affect the response.

If a young college man and a male companion are seated at a table in a restaurant and a beautiful girl of similar age passes by and smiles invitingly, the direction of the response is easily predictable, as well as the speed with which it will be made. Now consider this same young man in the same restaurant at the same table except that

. . . the direction of the response is easily predictable. . . .

instead of a male companion he has his "best girl" with him. When the same beautiful girl passes by and smiles invitingly the response will undoubtedly be quite different than in the first situation.

The stimulus in both instances was identical. The circumstances under which it was received differed. In both situations the young man's experiences with similar stimuli in the past would certainly have been reflected upon. He would have considered the circumstances surrounding the immediate stimulus with those surrounding the receipt of past similar stimuli; in both instances he would have evaluated the satisfactions received from responses to similar past experiences and he would in both illustrations have compared his goals or objectives at the time of receipt of the new stimulus with those held in the past.

This simple set of illustrations bypasses other important parts of the framework in which stimuli are received. Two mental phenomena commonly called "frame of reference" and "mood" may be used as examples.

The frame of reference for a given type of stimulus will vary among individuals. It is in essence the conceptual boundaries within which a given stimulus falls. A diamond which weighs an ounce is considered huge, because the accumulated experience regarding existing diamonds warrants the deduction that few are larger. On the other hand, one would conclude that a piece of limestone weighing one ounce is relatively small. Considering diamonds and limestone, there is a high degree of agreement of frames of reference among individuals.

When working with human beings in areas where there might be a wide divergence in frame of reference about a single topic, one must consider what the prevailing framework is likely to be. A pattern of behavior or a given action which one individual perceives as impossible may be considered easy by another. Men rarely if ever achieve any goal which they believe to be impossible of attainment. They usually choose courses of action which they consider within their range of capabilities. The range of capabilities of any one person in an area therefore usually is limited by his personal conception of his range, regardless of his innate or true capabilities.

Mood is the emotional state of an individual at any given time. It may be illustrated briefly by reference to certain words descriptive of moods which have gained general use. These include elation, depression, lassitude, and receptiveness. Mood is often influenced by fatigue, boredom, comfort or discomfort, recent experiences, and hundreds of other situational stimuli received at the conscious or subconscious level.

Another perhaps even more important set of variables goes to determine the sort of response that will be made to a stimulus. Considerable effort has been devoted to the difference between the instinctive or conditioned reflex responses of animals and the rational or thinking response of man. One might have gathered that the *quality* of the human response was a more or less standard product, whereas in truth the quality of the response may be subject to tremendous variation within the species, and for that matter, within the individual.

One sort of response is called nonrational or emotional. It is based upon the thinking process as previously described, but it operates at a fairly primitive level where the responses are made in respect to how we "feel" about something — whether we are pleased or gratified, whether the response creates a feeling of well-being, etc. Also, some of them might be made because of fear of consequences or even to avoid facing an unpleasant series of thoughts.

All humans have these emotions and react emotionally on many levels. As the individual finds himself higher in the scale of intelligence and education he becomes more and more capable of making "intellectual" choices. This is the highest of human abilities and perhaps it would be fair to say that the development of this type of response is the true aim of civilization, culture, and education.

It is a fact of human behavior that no matter how high a person may have risen in his ability to make rational decisions, they are certain to be colored or modified by his emotional background. Such qualities give man many of his "human"· characteristics and can never be duplicated by an "electronic brain."

Because of all these factors which enter into the interpretive process, many different responses may result from the same stimulus in a group situation. For example, when a chairman of a group asks for volunteers, some respond while others do not. The stimulus was the same. Individuals interpreted this stimulus — the request — in terms of their past experiences, evaluations, and expectancies before accepting or rejecting the request. One person may interpret the request as an opportunity for new experience, a challenging job to try. Another person may regard the request as a means by which the chairman is asking for someone to do his work for him again!

Since man responds to interpretation of the stimulus rather than the stimulus directly, he may hear the request in one group and accept it and hear a similar request in

. . . his rational decisions are certain to be colored by his emotional background.

another group and reject it. Because he can think abstractly, he can bring his past and his conception of the future to bear on each stimulus he receives and act according to his judgments to maximize the goals for which he is striving.

Man, born into this world an acting being, goes through life responding to innumerable stimuli in each of his waking hours. Each of these stimulus-interpretation-response complexes is a unit act, and as such represents a minimum unit of human behavior. It consists essentially of two parts; an end or goal to be attained, and a means or technique for its attainment.

VALUES, THE BASIS OF ACTION

The ends or goals of any man's actions and the actions themselves are not randomly determined. There is a consistency in them. The framework which provides this consistency is what is known as his value orientation or, very loosely, his philosophy of life.

A man develops this value system in various ways. Regardless of how it develops, it is essentially a mental categorization of ends and means which are evaluated as acceptable or unacceptable in varying degrees.

Members of the same culture and the same groups tend to have similar value systems but the unique experiences of all individuals result in many differences in emphasis which they place on any given end or means. Group action takes place when ends sought are commonly espoused by members and are of relative importance to them. The means used, as well as the ends, must be acceptable to the group as a whole.

Some values held by an individual are instilled in his thought patterns by the culture; they are accepted from the value systems of others. Examples of this are found everywhere. Children receive certain stimuli and in the process of responding, the parent assigns good or bad to alternative response choices. One of the reasons why others have such a disproportionately large influence on the younger child is that the young child is constantly being exposed to completely new stimuli and lacks the experiences from which to make his own interpretations. He is much more susceptible to acceptance of the interpretations of others. In the presence of a parent, each new stimulus is followed immediately by another stimulus, i.e., the suggestion of the parent as to the proper response.

As the individual becomes more experienced and has been exposed to many more stimuli toward which he has responded, he builds up a reservoir of alternatives in his memory. He builds a system of values based upon his own judgments of the relative good and bad of his past experiences. These experiences include the evaluations of others. The degree to which an individual accepts value judgments of others as his own ranges all the way from complete uncritical acceptance of another's evaluation to complete rejection of outside evaluations. The individual more readily accepts the evaluations of others whom he knows well and respects and with whose values he agrees. When we say that one individual knows another, we're basically saying that he is relatively aware of the other's past experiences, his ends and objectives, and accepted techniques for attaining his goals.

The individual more readily accepts the evaluations of others whom he respects. . . .

It is recognized that because of inherent qualities, individuals have varying abilities to act in given mental and physical ways. This difference in inherited capabilities is only one factor in accounting for differences in human behavior. The experience of the individual is also of great importance in determining how he responds in any situation. The relative importance of these two types of influence in determining individual behavior cannot be stated precisely.

We accumulate experience from the many people with whom we have contact, the groups to which we belong, the reading we do, and from all the stimuli we receive and retain. Each of us has had experiences that are different — unique experiences that helped create our individuality.

It has been pointed out that man has values concerning both the goals he wants to attain and the means that are acceptable to him in that goal attainment. Because of our different cultural backgrounds, the different group experiences that we have had, and the unique experiences in which each of us has participated, it is relatively easy to see why there are so many differences among us as individuals. We may have different values — different things are acceptable and important to us. Even if we believe in basically the same things, we may attach varying importance to individual items within our accepted pattern of values. Even if we believe the same basic goals are important, we may not agree on the best, most enjoyable, or even acceptable method or means to attain a given goal.

It is within this broad framework of values with regard to the ends or objectives we want to attain and the acceptable means to attain those ends that we begin to seek answers as to what makes people act — what motivates them — what makes them "tick." Why does one person seem to drag his feet at every new suggestion? Why does another always seem to have to be the center of group activity? Why is being recognized as a leader so important to another?

MOTIVATIONS

There are many theories extant as to the motivations of men, and the authors are aware that these many explanations exist. They are acquainted with much more sophisticated explanations of human wants than the "four wishes" of W. I. Thomas,[1] but for the purposes of this book they find the classification a useful one in pointing out the general lines along which motivations flow. It will be accepted that man, wherever he is found — in the jungles of Africa, in the Arctic or on Main Street, U.S.A. — has four basic desires which Thomas has pointed out. The four "wishes" are security, new experience, recognition, and response. These obviously constitute an oversimplification and are not specific wishes, but rather a broad social-psychological classification of the various types of social desires of individuals. In the following descriptions of the wishes, it should be remembered that none exist in a pure form, but the combinations in various degree always exist.

Security. All wishes or desires stem from man's ability to think, and the way he satisfies these wishes is based upon his basic value orientation. He may place a high value on security. If he does, most of the goals which he accepts will be those which he thinks will give him immediate or ultimate security.

The individual's wish for security might be satisfied by temporal material things such as food, shelter, and clothing, and adequate reserves of wealth to secure these in the future. This wish might be satisfied by spiritual beliefs in the hereafter, and by the individual's feeling that he had a chance of going to a desirable locale after death. Whether or not such beliefs could be grounded in reality is immaterial since when men consider situations to be real, they act as if they were.

---

[1] W. I. Thomas, *The Unadjusted Girl*, Little, Brown, Boston, 1923.

Still others satisfy the security wish by being accepted into groups which they consider to be important to their well being. They find security in belonging. Security to many group members means a feeling that the group will behave in a regular, routine fashion. Such a member feels that if changes are made in group functioning, they will be brought about slowly, and he, as an individual, will not be thrust into a new situation rapidly and without warning. His security is relative to the degree of his feeling of acceptance by the group.

New Experience. This wish or motivation may be satisfied by seeking contacts with new people, seeking out or creating new social situations in which to become involved, learning and accepting new and different responsibilities, and learning to play new and different roles. A person highly motivated by this wish would jump at the opportunity to take on a difficult committee assignment or try a new group technique. A new and difficult social situation might well act as a challenge to this individual rather than create a feeling of insecurity or frustration.

Recognition. The wish for recognition is expressed in the desire of the individual to "be somebody" in the eyes of his fellows. This wish is so well expressed in our culture and so generally understood that little discussion is necessary. Each individual feels the need to be considered important by his fellow men. This need arises, as was pointed out earlier, because man with his unique thinking ability

self

Each individual feels the need to be considered important by his fellow men.

conceptualizes himself in relation to others and he has mental images of what others think of him. Since we live in a highly competitive culture, people vie for status as well as wealth. Wealth may become simply a device for providing status and recognition. Being known as an important person, getting one's name in the paper, working on a job which has high prestige, and other ways too obvious to mention are all ways of satisfying the need for recognition.

In the ideal formal democratic group, where ideas are accepted on their merit, individuals are ascribed status on the basis of their ability to create ideas rather than on other bases. Thus the pure democratic group provides a totally different framework within which individuals may achieve status or recognition.

Response. The wish for response is the desire to be wanted; the feeling that others enjoy one's association and wish to continue it. This wish differs from the wish for recognition in that the individual is not as concerned about his prestige and recognition as a matter of public knowledge and public record. As a minimum for response satisfaction, the reference groups which the individual considers significant must accept him as a person and indicate their satisfaction with his being one of them. An individual satisfies his need for response by gaining acceptance with a small number of individuals, his peers, who know him on a primary face-to-face basis and accept him as a person for what he is, including his foibles.

In any society one can find those who satisfy their need for response by accepting the menial tasks which need to be performed, such as washing dishes, and get satisfaction from being needed and from associating with others while performing these tasks. A person satisfying this need for response is satisfied by the fact that others recognize him as a personality and empathize with him, understand him, and accept him. He revels in being liked by others. Even those who chiefly value status also value the response of those about them.

The social interactions related to satisfaction of need

for response are usually much more intimate than those of recognition. In the desire for response, people may seek relationships such as love, affection, respect, a feeling of being wanted, and belonging with and to other people. The need for response is often satisfied by a feeling of acceptance as a total person. An individual likes to feel that others like to have him around. He likes to feel that others confide in him and seek his help and advice. He interacts with others in solving their and his little personal problems. Under these circumstances he is satisfying his need for response.

Individuals make different choices regarding the extent to which they attempt to satisfy these various wishes. The choices are usually based on the personal values arrived at through interpretations of past experiences in situations which involved earlier efforts to satisfy these wishes.

All individuals experience all of these wishes in varying degrees of intensity. Some people have a stronger desire for satisfaction of one or of another of these wishes. The need for satisfaction of this wish continuously assumes precedence over others in such a person.

If one accepts the proposition that the actions of human beings are oriented around the satisfaction of these wishes, one is led to ask why men the world over attempt to satisfy these wishes in so many different ways. The over-simplified answer to this is that the culture in which men find themselves sets the boundaries within which these wishes must be satisfied, and the unique experiences of each individual determines the emphasis he will place on the satisfaction of each wish.

These basic wishes may be fulfilled in many different ways. In many instances, motivations arising from them can contribute to group productivity. In other cases they may hinder group productivity. The wish for recognition may be fulfilled by doing a given job well. For this, recognition is given by fellow members. However, if an individual cannot get this kind of positive recognition from the group, he may turn to unacceptable behavior to gain attention. Thus the frustrated group member may turn to being a "cut-up" or playboy, a blocker, or a discussion monopolizer.

The group member that feels thwarted at gaining new experience within the acceptable group value system and action framework may fulfill his wish by inventing new techniques to slow up or disrupt group operation. This may give release to his desire for new experience. In some instances, when an individual is not having new experiences, he drops out of the group.

The individual who feels he is not receiving the proper response from group members may find one or two other persons who share his attitude. They may form a tight-knit clique and turn their interests and actions toward themselves, rather than the group and its activities.

He may invent new techniques to slow up or disrupt group discussion, decision, or action.

When group members and leaders recognize that the need for individual satisfactions exist in their groups, methods can be used which will move the group toward its goals and at the same time bring satisfaction to individuals. *Group productivity is greatest in those groups where techniques are used which simultaneously further the attainment of the group goals and bring fulfillment of the wishes of individual members.*

Although group members may have been born and reared in the same community, they may join a group for many different reasons; they are trying to satisfy various personal desires and needs. Out of these different value orientations, different felt needs, and different desires for goal fulfillment, they must find common interests, motivations, patterns of interaction, and personal relations that will enable them to move effectively toward wish satisfaction and goal fulfillment within the group structure.

REASONS FOR GROUP AFFILIATION

In his quest to satisfy his needs and wants, man has found that many of them are best satisfied through group affiliation and action. If the members of various groups are asked why they joined, they will give many different answers. Some might have joined because membership in the group will enhance their status. Others joined because of a value placed on service — they wanted to help other people and feel this group gives them this opportunity. Another person may have joined a group because he feels he may make some business contacts that he feels in the end may make him some money. There are other kinds of personal-gain motivations.

Some may have joined almost purely from tradition — their mother or father was an active member and it was just expected that they would also be a member. Others joined because all their friends belong and being a member of the group is a way to be with their friends. A few joined because

Still others join groups because "it's good for business."

they are lonely people and they think they might make some more intimate contacts and perhaps make some friends. Others joined what they feel is a "different" group — they can escape from some of the restrictions and frustrations of everyday and other group life. Of course, many joined because of the specific activity of the group: politics, gardening, photography, great books, or whatever has high priority as an activity for them. Others joined because their boss or boss's wife suggested that belonging to this group is "a good thing to do" if one wants to "get ahead." In any group there may be a tremendous diversity of interests and motivations for belonging.

When one is aware of this diversity, it becomes easier to understand why certain groups have difficulties in agreeing upon goals and objectives and the methods which they will use to achieve them. It is recognized that it is impossible to know all there is to know about group members. However, if one has some understanding of them as individuals, what their basic drives and motivations are, and what needs they are trying to fulfill, one is in a better position to treat them as individuals, find areas of common agreement, find challenges that will motivate them, and better understand why they act as they do. Basic understanding of fellow group members is one of the first steps in any individual's becoming a productive group member.

. . . . many basic desires are best satisfied through group activity.

Since people feel that many of their basic desires are best satisfied through group activity, one might expect that everyone is interested in group activity and that groups are fulfilling their needs. It is not that simple. Many people do not belong to formal groups. Many members do not actively participate. Other groups do not really satisfy their members' needs or fulfill their goal expectations, even though the members participate actively.

BLOCKS TO PARTICIPATION

There are many blocks to full participation in groups. A potential member may not know of the existence of groups having goals and objectives similar to his own. He may know of a group and accept its goals and objectives, but disapprove of the means used to attain them. He may have a feeling of insecurity about groups, a concern as to whether or not the group will accept him. He may fear that he lacks the human relations skills to get along with the other group members or he may feel inferior to them for other reasons such as his status, educational background, or even his clothing.

A person may be hesitant to join a group because he is not sure of the groups' expectations of its members. He may feel that the other group members are so much more skilled in human relations or know so much more about the subject under discussion that he will have to refrain from participating. There are many other blocks and frustrations. Many are operative at the conscious level in the individual, still others may be subconscious.

In order to become efficient group members, individuals should study themselves and try objectively to cope with their blocks and frustrations. A responsibility of all members in a mature democratic group is to help others to analyze themselves objectively so that they can overcome their blocks and frustrations and participate more effectively in the ongoing group process.

ADJUSTMENTS TO BLOCKS

There are many different ways to help adjust these blocks or wish frustrations, many of which are not at the rational, conscious level. Man thinks in terms of abstractions and tends to constantly organize his experiences with the universe around him. He therefore must have some rationale or mental escape for any failures in his attempts to attain goals within that experience world. The ways in which he does this are called *adjustments*.

Aggression. One common adjustment to frustration — the blocking of progress toward some desired goal — is aggression. When one's ideas are not accepted or when he as a person is not accepted, he may strike back blindly. He may show his aggression by gestures, words, or even physical violence. He may feel or say: "Well, you people are not interested in *good* ideas;" or "Boy, what a snobbish person he is, he won't even talk to me." He may turn this aggression inward and condemn himself: "You stupid fool, why did you say that?"

Compensation. Sometimes an individual adjusts to wish frustration by this device. If he is frustrated in reaching a given goal, he may divert his energies into another field by substituting another goal. If as a group member he has difficulty in communicating in group discussion, he may refrain from comment during discussion but devote a tremendous amount of energy to the "leg work" in carrying out the actions decided upon by the group. In some cases this type of compensation-substitution is a rational recognition of one's unique abilities. However, many times it is used as an excuse for not trying to improve understandings and skills to overcome this wish blockage.

Rationalization. Many adjust to wish frustration by the process of rationalization. If one finds it difficult to attain a goal, he may unconsciously explain the situation away by denying to himself that he ever wanted to attain it. Thus, when he was defeated for an office in an organization, he tells himself that after all, it is not an important office and he really didn't have time to do a very good job even if he had been elected. If he has a frustrating experience leading a discussion, he may adjust by making the unconscious excuse that the group members really are not very good discussants and, besides, discussions never get any place anyway. Rationalization usually takes place at the unconscious level.

Identification. This adjustment may take the form of living through the lives of others by participating vicariously in their successful attainment rather than seeking satisfactions in unknown activities. Those who adjust through identification often imitate the behavior and mannerisms of the person with whom they identify themselves. In terms of this adjustment one may be able to understand the joy or sorrow of one person because of success or failure of another person with whom he identifies. Also, one may be able to understand why a given person seems satisfied with mediocre levels of attainment for himself — he really receives his rewards from the attainments of another. Other group ramifications of this adjustment can be seen by the reader.

Idealization. This form of adjustment is closely related to identification. It is the adjustment to such feelings as one's own inadequacy by over-evaluating himself — his ability, attainment, importance. He may also idealize other individuals and their attainments. Thus he may compensate for an unconscious feeling of inadequacy by trying to convince himself that he is really a good group member. An individual is idealizing when he assigns greater value to his contributions to the group than the group as a whole would assign to them. Idealization may be of one's own behavior or of another person's behavior. When an individual over-evaluates other's behavior, he ceases to be objective about group function.

. . . he tells himself that after all, it is not an important office. . . .

Displacement. This is the adjustment which takes place when an individual transfers the feelings he has for one person to another. It often accompanies idealization. If one person idealizes another and that individual does something of which the idealizer does not approve, he may blame someone else. Often displacement takes place because the individual doing the displacing finds it more convenient to express himself to one person than to another. A person may be angry at his boss but say nothing to him; instead he may go home in the evening and vent his spleen on his wife and children.

Projection. This adjustment to wish frustration is one wherein the individual transfers to another his own feelings of inadequacies or frustrations. If a person has been unsuccessful in his role as a discussion leader he may project the blame on the group for not playing their proper roles. Or if group member A has not expressed himself well to group member B, he may project his own inadequacy to B by accusing him of lacking an open mind.

Conversion. Conversion is the transfer of energy after or during a wish frustration into some physical symptom or complaint. In extreme cases individuals may actually develop the symptoms of a physical ailment in this adjustment to wish frustration. A person who may have wanted to do a good job as a meeting leader may actually become ill if the job doesn't turn out the way he wanted it. All mothers are familiar with this adjustment as displayed by children; innumerable mothers have seen their youngsters develop stomach-aches on the day they were scheduled to have examinations at school. In many instances the symptoms will be very real.

Regression. The adjustment known as regression is a process of retreating from an existing complex situation to a simpler one. When an individual finds a situation too complex, he may revert in his behavior to a less mature approach in anticipation of being dealt with on this level. In its more

. . . he may revert to a less mature approach in anticipation of being dealt with on this level.

socially acceptable forms, the individual using this form of adjustment audibly wishes for, or actually tries to create, a simpler situation. A commonly found example of this form in group situations is the oft-heard expression of individuals in growing groups that they wish the groups were smaller and more intimate. This results from the fact that most people feel more competent to communicate in primary group situations with people whom they know on a more intimate basis. Probably the most commonly observed form of this adjustment is that certain group members pout when they don't get their own way — a regression to a childhood form of coping with this type of frustration.

Negativism. This adjustment is a common one. It is the behavior pattern in which a frustrated individual responds to all subsequent alternatives in a negative way. Children frequently refuse to do anything if they can't do what they wanted. "If I can't pitch I won't play."

Fantasy. This adjustment involves the imagining of situations in which one's goals are achieved when frustration takes place. Daydreaming is the common term applied to this form of adjustment.

Many reactions that one sees in people may at first be

difficult to understand. They become more understandable when analyzed in the framework of wish frustration and adjustment to that frustration. The plea again is for rational analysis of self and one's actions. One needs to predict the possible frustration of others and conduct oneself so these frustrations can be minimized for all. In a mature group, leaders may help group members to understand their frustrations and the adjustments they are making to those frustrations. It is within this framework that they will mature most rapidly as group members. Otherwise, the group may spend most of its time and energy in keeping members from being frustrated and have little time and energy left for productive decision making and action.

Most adjustments are complex, and it is difficult to spell out mutually exclusive definitions. It should be recognized that any occurrence may cause frustration for someone. Often because of conflicting or competitive interests, goal satisfaction to one individual means frustration to another.

It is of some interest to note that extremes of behavior as seen in excessive adjustment can be readily identified with the well-known forms of mental disease. For example, hysteria corresponds to excessive conversion, while the sociopath is an example of excessive aggression. One may recognize extreme regression in depressive psychosis and unlimited fantasy in the way the schizophrenic loses contact with reality. Opinion is divided as to whether these mental diseases are in actuality exaggerations of the frustration adjustments of normal persons or whether they have simply developed along similar patterns.

Adjustments which people make to frustrations are not necessarily *good* or *bad*. Because individuals live in an organized society in which certain freedoms to act without concern for others have been relinquished for the common good, it is inevitable that some wishes and desires will be blocked. In a democratic society, the minority position always involves frustration. Frustrations are an intrinsic and normal part of the interaction of human beings. The group member or group leader who recognizes this and attempts to create social interaction patterns within his group which will minimize frustrations will find that group morale will remain higher and the group will move more rapidly toward the achievement of its goals.

Group members need to recognize that there are both destructive and useful effects in the kinds of adjustments which one can make to goal frustrations. Adjustments such as rationalization can be used as a constant escape from the reality of the social situations in which one finds oneself. However, if this adjustment is used intelligently it provides an "escape" around the goal blockage which allows him to go on to do other constructive activities.

On the other extreme, such adjustments as regression or aggression, while they may give the individual immediate release from the tensions built up by the goal blockage, nearly always have adverse effects on group morale. When individuals or groups are blocked in the attainment of a goal, they may either change their attitudes and their goals,

. . . they may strive to change the circumstances which caused the blockage in the first place.

or strive to change the circumstances which caused the blockage in the first place. As members become more skilled at recognizing the factors which cause blockage or frustration and the kinds of adjustments made in these situations, they can choose rationally to make those adjustments which require the least expenditure of time and emotional energy. This leads to greater individual motivation, greater personal satisfactions with the group and its activities and greater group productivity.

GROUP FORMATION

Group formation and participation, including individual motivations, blocks, and adjustments, is illustrated in Figure 5.1. It is a complex process by which an aggregate of people with a wide variety of individual goals, values, skills, and blocks to group participation mold themselves into a productive group. Because each aggregate is unique it is nearly impossible to describe the total social process of group formation. But there are certain basic necessities common to all group development and certain essentials which must exist before a group will be formed.

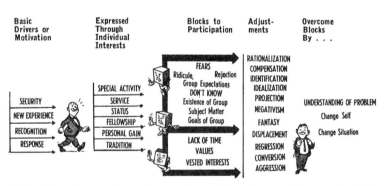

FIG. 5.1 — Group formation and participation includes individual motivations, blocks, and adjustments.

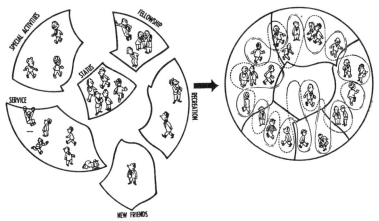

FIG. 5.2 — Minimum essentials of group formation.

First, it must be discovered — through communication — what the individual interests of the various persons are, and which of these individual interests are held in common by most of the potential group members. When people get together to form a group to achieve a certain goal or set of goals, it is assumed that they expect to get the active participation of those involved. If members are going to give continued effort to any group, they must feel that through such participation they will be able to satisfy at least those individual interests which are held in common and also that some of their personal needs will be satisfied incidentally and without conflict with others' interests.

The minimum essentials of group formation are represented graphically in Figure 5.2. The left portion of the diagram illustrates individuals with different priorities of individual interests. If these individuals are to be formed into a group, common interests must be established. There must emerge the belief that the individuals possess some interests in common and that the group formed represents the potential of fulfilling those interests (illustrated by the right portion of the diagram).

In democratic groups, it is the responsibility of members to become aware of these individual variations and to make contributions which move the group to rational adjustments to frustrations.

MEMBERSHIP RENEWAL

With this rudimentary consideration of group formation and membership we can move on to a brief discussion of membership renewal. In a culture such as ours, with great vertical and horizontal mobility, there is apt to be frequent need to renew or enlarge membership. Some organizations have a built-in declining membership. The college fraternity loses members through graduation. The Junior Chamber of Commerce sets a maximum age limit for members. For such groups, renewal of membership is a constant need and requires a considerable expenditure of effort. Many communities sponsor organizations known as "newcomers clubs," the principal purpose of which is to introduce recent arrivals to the group life of the community. In such a group, membership renewal becomes the principal goal. Even the most stable of groups are liable to find themselves with a membership declining, either in numbers or in interest. They must go about adding to the membership with an attitude quite similar to that called for in group formation.

UPGRADING MEMBERSHIP

Another aspect of group membership is the continuing one of upgrading. There is usually a certain uniformity, or homogeneity, in group membership. People tend to congregate into groups made up of others with similar education, status, class, occupation, religion, likes, dislikes, etc. Exceptions will be noted, but this is a general rule. Even the leadership tends to come from the same level, for we are as suspicious of superiority as we are bored with inferiority. Within any group, however, there is still a wide spread in group skills, in resource potential, and in many of the other qualities which go to make up good group membership. Upgrading may mean the exploitation of this degree of heterogeneity, or it may mean going outside what may be considered the normal range of members to secure individuals with special ability.

Often groups underestimate the group affiliation interest and desires of people who have exceptional knowledge or skills. Many people with these special attributes would be interested in becoming "regular" group members or playing special roles in groups if only they understood the group's goals and means and were asked to join.

Some groups do not attempt to upgrade their membership because consciously, or unconsciously, they don't want people with greater knowledge, abilities, or skills in their group. They fear that these new members might upset the status structure. This point of view denies the possibility of the potential for individual and group growth from internal stimulation and higher group standards made possible by adding high caliber new members.

RESOURCE PERSONNEL

Related to upgrading group membership is the effective use of consultants, or resource personnel, by groups. Seldom does any group contain experts or specialists in all the fields they may wish to explore. Common sense suggests that liberal use be made of persons with special knowledge or skills rather than proceeding on a basis of pooled ignorance. It has already been suggested that upon occasion such specialized help may be integrated into the group. In many other cases it will obviously be impossible, and sometimes not even desirable.

The frequency and intelligence with which groups use specialists may be one evidence of maturity. Resource personnel are available in an ever-widening circle of specialties. Their talents may be general or limited, but a little effort and ingenuity can usually turn up the knowledge sought.

6.

The Internal Dynamics of Groups

WE HAVE SEEN how each individual brings certain characteristics which are peculiarly his own to the group. These include his interests, his abilities, his desires or wishes, as well as his blocks and frustrations and his adjustments to them — in other words his "personality." We have come to think of all these items of individuality as *forces* which contribute to the dynamics of the group. In addition to these forces (which may be said to be the property of the persons involved), certain other forces seem to develop as a result of interaction between individuals. These are a property of the group as a whole. The summation, integration, and resolution of all these forces have been labeled the *internal dynamics* of the group.

If use of the term *dynamics* tends to become repetitious it is because it has developed as the only word which connotes all the things implied in its use — that is, the energies and forces derived, both from the individuals and from their interaction with each other, and the summation and resolution of these forces into active as opposed to static behavior.

It will be remembered from Chapter 4, where the outline of ideas concerning group behavior was discussed, that these ideas were divided into those involving the group, the goals, and the means. The internal dynamics, under that framework, was regarded as a function of the group and will continue to be so regarded. However, much of what will later be considered under goals (Chapter 8) and techniques (Chapters 9 and 10) also comes under the heading of internal dynamics. The dynamic qualities which go to make up group action are not solely the property of the group but also are an essential part of goal selection and orientation as well as of methods.

FIGURE 6.1 — Internal dynamics of groups.

These ideas cannot be neatly pigeonholed into specific compartments. No matter how the various components are labeled, there will always be cross-reacting, overlapping, and spill-over. For that reason the forces of the group which go to make up the internal dynamics will be discussed under a series of subheads which do not necessarily carry equal value or at times even seem to be related. Certainly they will not be mutually exclusive. The list will be far from exhaustive, but will be detailed enough to point the way for the reader to create his own concept for its expansion. We will consider group size, group atmosphere, group identification, and qualities of homogeneous or heterogeneous composition. Also under study will be communication within the group, participation, the leadership pattern, and the kind of human relation skills present. The definition of roles, the kinds of roles needed for productivity, the objectives sought, and the activities chosen will all come under discussion in this chapter. All these will be influenced by the standards of operation and the degrees of social controls under which the group functions. Finally, the matter of group evaluation, while a specific force, will need to encompass all the foregoing aspects.

These various factors exist in all groups and many of them are immediately apparent. At any given time certain of them may be so obscure as to be considered latent, if present at all. Often they will be operating at such a low level of consciousness that only definitive objective consideration of the part they play will bring them into observable focus. For that reason a series of questions to be asked regarding any group has been included under each of the several subheads.

The forces which will be described are at the disposal of all group members as well as specified group leaders. Recalling our concept of leadership and recognizing that in the democratic group all members carry both responsibility and capacity for leadership, this subject will not be specifically discussed further in this chapter. Along with goals and techniques its elaboration is carried out elsewhere.

With the above qualifications we can now consider a selected battery of forces. Their general nature can be indicated by a commonly understood word or phrase expounded and extended for our purposes by the discussion. This somewhat detailed discussion has two purposes: (1) reporting the general principles regarding each as modern research has revealed them; and (2) the establishment of a framework for the analysis of groups such as our own.

ATMOSPHERE

Group atmosphere is the pervading mood, tone, or feeling that permeates the group.

To begin with, the actual physical setting in which the group operates is important in helping determine the group atmosphere. The lighting, ventilation, or even the drabness or brightness of the room may be contributing factors to group atmosphere. The seating arrangement is also important. Seating in a circular or elliptical pattern where everyone can be seen and no persons are in physically dom-

. . . people may distrust each other, their motives, or their willingness to really say what they think.

inant positions may be valuable in creating a friendly, permissive atmosphere.

Such a simple consideration as making sure that each member of the group has not only met each of the other members but has had opportunity to know a little about them is important. Addressing people by their preferred names can improve group atmosphere.

When individuals meet and work together they no longer behave only as individual units but respond as a collective whole to the prevailing group atmosphere. In the groups with warm, permissive, democratic atmosphere, there seems to be greater work motivation and greater satisfaction — and the individuals and groups are more productive. There seems to be less discontent, frustration, and aggression in these groups. There is more friendliness, cordiality, cooperation, and "we-feeling." There also seems to be more individual thinking, more creativeness, and better motivation. Participation in decision making in this democratic permissive atmosphere seems to facilitate the development of the individual motivations that serve to increase member productivity and morale.

A group member's behavior is determined to a considerable extent by his perception of the reaction of the group toward him. The individual who feels secure, who perceives himself as having adequate group skills, more often takes the lead in group activities. The total resources of the group can be tapped more adequately when all individuals feel free to contribute and question as the group moves toward its goals. Motivation and morale reach high levels in a democratic permissive atmosphere where there is active participation of both the leaders and members of the group.

The atmosphere may be one of fear or suspicion; fear of being ridiculed, made fun of, or rejected. There may be a feeling of suspicion in the sense that people distrust each other, their motives, or their willingness to really say what they think. The group atmosphere may be aggressive — everyone at each other's throat. The atmosphere may be apathetic — no life or vitality, with everyone waiting for someone else to do or say something.

On the other hand, the atmosphere of a group can be friendly and warm. It can be permissive — where everyone feels free to express himself honestly and participate in group activity for a free and open exchange of ideas and feelings.

There can be an authoritarian atmosphere. The responsibility is with the authority and no one may participate or initiate action except at the dictate of the authoritarian leader. It is presumed that the authority knows best what the group should believe and do. Group member behavior is *directed* toward the authority's predetermined ends.

There can be a democratic atmosphere. Leadership is shared by all, and individuals strive to recognize and play roles needed for group productivity. The responsibility of the formal leader and other group members is that of creating conditions — including group atmosphere — under which group members are best able to work together to accomplish chosen ends.

A crucial stage of atmosphere creation is the opening of a meeting. The way the leader introduces himself and the subject, the length of time he speaks, how dogmatically he speaks, and the spelling out of the general role expectations of group members can all be important factors contributing to a good group atmosphere.

Crucial stage of atmosphere creation is at the opening of a meeting.

Underlying the establishment of a warm, friendly, permissive feeling are certain fundamental considerations that all group members should have. There must be a basic belief in the value of the individual — a sincere belief in the dignity of man and an honest respect for each man's point of view. Along with this basic belief, group members should develop a social sensitivity toward the group and its members. This social sensitivity (the understanding of individual personality traits and social interactions) should enable group members to determine and respond to the concerns, desires, and needs of the group and its members. The ability to see beyond one's own needs to the wider range of needs of other group members and the group as a whole may well be the most important step in the establishment of a permissive group atmosphere.

What About YOUR Group?

1. Is the physical setting, room arrangement, lighting, and ventilation that which will contribute to a good social atmosphere?
2. Is there an atmosphere of permissiveness, warmth, and good feeling, or hostility, suspicion, aggression, and apathy?
3. Are people helped to feel a part of the group, or are they forced to feel isolated?
4. Does your group understand the difference between authoritarianism, democratic, and laissez-faire atmosphere and leadership?

5. Is there cooperative sharing among the members?
6. Do you try to imagine yourselves in the other fellow's shoes?
7. Is discussion on a rational and objective basis or subjective and emotional?

COMMUNICATION PATTERNS

We may think of communication as the process whereby we convey ideas, sentiments, or beliefs to others. Though we usually envision communication in terms of speech or language we may also communicate by visual representations, gestures, and imitation. Language, however, constitutes the chief form of social interaction between humans. Through this medium we learn to know people, share experiences, ideas, sentiments, and beliefs. Hence we define, diagnose, and solve our common problems.

Many group problems result from the inability of leaders or group members to communicate with other group members. We mean to say one thing but perhaps say quite another. We assume everyone understands us or our point of view. The same words may mean different things to different people. A slight inflection or emphasis may be

. . . we may communicate by visual representations, gestures, and imitation.

interpreted by others much differently than was intended. The meaning of a facial expression or a body gesture may be completely misinterpreted. It seems that the old axiom about army orders applies equally well to group communication, "If it can be misunderstood, it will be misunderstood."

In heterogeneous groups — where there are people with different backgrounds, occupations, formal education, and levels of communication skills — it is particularly important that each group member makes sure he is communicating with all other group members.

Group members tend to feel left out and unsure of themselves when they do not have two-way communication. Even when acts of hostility are communicated, there seems to be less resentment between the sender and the receiver when there is firm understanding on both sides.

Where there is the desire to change the attitudes and subsequent behavior of group members, two-way communication in formal or informal discussions tends to be more effective than lecture or direct order from above.

A group member is more productive when he feels that he has access to relevant information. Of special importance is communication on matters that directly affect him and the definition of his role.

Those groups that are most productive have a more adequate communication network set up than those that are less productive. There is higher group participation, productivity, and satisfaction when members feel they have the right to enter into discussion and where means are provided for adequate give and take between leaders and other group members.

Successful supervisors and leaders often achieve their results by paying attention not only to the members as individuals, but to the relationships, interactions, and communications within the group.

When formal communications are suppressed or ignored, informal lines of communication usually appear. In organizations where there is dominating leadership the informal organization structures that arise often have goals that conflict with the goals of the formal group structure. For instance, a subgroup that feels its lines of communication are blocked may take up the goal of making it difficult for the leader or getting rid of him.

In most group situations a decrease of interaction will bring about a decrease in the strength of interpersonal feelings and sentiments and will decrease member identity with the group. In groups that have a rigid status system, communication between status levels seems to serve as a substitute for real mobility toward higher levels. The results of many studies show the necessity of trying to communicate in the language that other group members can understand and accept.

What About YOUR Group?

1. Does your group really work at insuring good communication within the group?

2. Are there definite means of communication that involve group members in goal setting, determination of means, and ongoing group activities?

3. Are there definite means of communication for sharing knowledge, plans, administrative decisions, etc.?

4. Is there really two-way communication or just one-way communication?

5. Does your group depend mainly on grapevine or informal communication?

6. Have weaknesses of the formal communication system encouraged the development of cliques with nongroup goal orientation?

7. Has enough information and knowledge been communicated to individuals and subgroups so that they may coordinate their activities with others effectively?

8. Do the formal leaders of your group have only a "the door is always open" policy or do they actively seek communication opportunities?

9. Do you often overestimate how much other group members really know or understand?

10. Do you depend heavily on written communication rather than personal communication?

11. How are you attempting to interpret your group and its activities to the parent organization or community?

PARTICIPATION

One of the most important internal forces in group participation is the personal and psychological involvement of individuals in the affairs of the group. We generally think of group participation as an overt, observable expression through speech or actions. However, there are many subtler behavior patterns in terms of gestures, attitudes, or manners that constitute participation. We often think of participation as member involvement through speaking and entering into the discussion. We may think in terms of the breadth of participation — how many group members take part. We may think again of the intensity of participation — how often various individuals take part or how emotionally involved they become.

We may think of participation patterns — how people respond to each other. When one person enters the discussion, is he usually followed by certain others? Do a few people monopolize the discussion, or is there opportunity for all to participate? Do we help everyone participate? Is

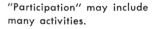

"Participation" may include many activities.

the participation pattern leader-centered or distributed throughout the group?

We may also think of participation in the sense of attending meetings, being on committees, being officers, helping finance, being on work groups, washing dishes, or writing publicity.

Research seems to indicate that individual and group productivity is related to the opportunities provided for member participation. These may include setting goals, deciding on means of attaining goals, and other aspects of discussion and decision making. Even when an individual's ideas do not agree with the final group decision, he is much happier when he has had an opportunity to participate and express himself in the decision-making process.

Participation in the analysis and decision-making process results in less resistance to change, lower turnover in group members, greater productivity, and greater satisfaction with the group and group membership. Decision making by representatives from the group, or careful explanation of decisions made by others are not acceptable substitutes for member participation in decisions. The more a member participates, the more favorable are his attitudes toward the group, and the greater his feeling of concern *for* and identity *with* the group.

Those members who participate the most are those who understand the basic purposes and function of the group, have clearly in mind the group's expectations of its members, feel secure in playing their member roles, and can see how their member roles contribute to the over-all purpose and functioning of the group. They also derive satisfaction from their participation.

What About YOUR Group?

1. What per cent of your members are really participating — attending meetings, serving on committees, taking part in group activities, speaking up in meetings, etc.?

2. Do you often decide it is easier to do it yourselves than to involve other people in helping?

3. How much attention are you paying to group participation in goal setting and other major group decisions?

4. Do you try consciously to find opportunity to involve people in meaningful group work situations?

5. Do you analyze your meeting procedures and activities from the point of view of the degree of meaningful member participation you may expect? Might other techniques accomplish your goals better and also facilitate much higher member participation?

6. Are you really willing to let members participate in policy decisions — or would you rather have a little less participation and feel in greater control of the situation?

7. Have you ever plotted the participation patterns in your group?

8. Do those people that participate too much realize what effect they are having on the group or other group members?

9. Have you really looked for alternative techniques you might use for solving your participation problems?

GROUP STANDARDS

Group standards may be defined as the level of performance acceptable to the group itself. Certain groups may be known for their high standards in relation to qualifications required to become a member. They may also set high standards of member conduct, participation in group activities, democratic decision making, and successful work completion. Other groups may be known for their sloppy meeting procedure, inept discussion, and jobs poorly or only partially done.

Group standards may be either implied or clearly stated. Nevertheless every group has its standards which, when enforced by social control, become important factors in determining the performance level of each member as well as the group as a whole. These standards become the group's expectations of its members and also determine the member's expectations of his group. Certain levels of expectations of other groups often then are judged in terms of the standards associated with the group.

Standards must be realistic — within the level of attainment of the group. They should be understood by all group members. Deviation from these expected performance standards, either above or below, is frowned on by the members, and the group sets up ways of securing conformance. If a member does not conform he is rejected. In most cases group members are more clearly in agreement on what the group norms or standards are than their observable behavior would indicate. Behavior is seldom in strict conformance to the ideal standard, but the limits of toleration are fairly well understood.

Some groups have found it advantageous to make both their expectations and their violations more explicit. For example, they might levy a small fine on a member for being

Deviation from expected performance standards is frowned on by other group members.

late to meetings to make explicit the standard of prompt attendance. A frank discussion of what the chairman of a committee has a right to expect of his committeemen, or vice versa, may lead to more clearly understood standards of committee operation.

In some cases failure to live up to group standards results from poor definition of the standards themselves. More frequently it is due to individuals not being aware of the standards or not understanding them.

. . . or certain individuals not being aware of or understanding the standards.

Group standards can be made more explicit and in many cases raised by looking objectively at either past performance or contemplated action and asking the group members if it is an acceptable level of performance.

In most cases, *higher* group standards are set when the *entire group* is involved in setting the standards as compared with standards being set by a small clique or an individual. Members have greater motivation to conduct themselves in keeping with those standards — to maintain their own conduct and to see that other group members maintain their conduct.

In terms of individual frustration or satisfaction, it is important that the standards are consistent — not rigidly enforced at one meeting and loosely at the next. This seems more important than the actual level at which the standards are set.

In general, the closer the individual comes to living up to all group standards or norms, the higher will be the group status of that individual, and his sense of satisfaction with his relationship.

What About YOUR Group?

1. Is there group involvement in setting your group standards?

2. Are the group standards well understood by all members?

3. As new group standard-setting situations arise, does the group attempt to make those standards explicit?

4. Are group discussion, human relations, participation, techniques, and progress evaluated against group standards?

5. Do your group members make known their expectations of the group — the standards expected from the group as a whole?

6. Are your group standards realistic?

7. Are your group standards evaluated periodically?

8. Is your group attempting to up-grade group standards realistically as it becomes more mature?

9. Does your group consider the expectations of the parent organization or community in setting its own group standards?

10. What sort of an example in living up to group standards is set by formal leaders and other key people in your group?

SOCIAL CONTROL

The means whereby the group secures conformity to the expectations of its group members is termed social control. This may take the form of rewards to group members for meeting group standards. Such rewards may include recognition before the group, election to office, being accorded a certain status, or being given some other tangible recognition such as a perfect-attendance pin. Other rewards are less tangible and may take the form of being accepted by the group, a feeling of response from other group members, a smile, a word, or a pat on the back.

Control may also be in the form of punishments. Censure, ridicule, rejection, destatusing, taking away privileges, or actual physical acts against the offender are examples of this type of control.

Every group has its group standards and enforces them by varying degrees of social control. Some groups rely mostly on incentives or rewards for control, others more on fear or punishment. If groups are to be productive, members need to know what the standards of the group are and the means used to enforce those standards — the methods of control. As pointed out, it seems to be important that the methods of control are recognized by group members and uniformly enforced — not rigidly enforced one time and very loosely enforced the next.

It is also important that social controls apply equally to all group members. This creates problems since there is seldom absolute conformity to any social norm. Thus control is brought into play, not so much by deviation from a norm, but by departure from the existing *degree* of obedience to the norm. The group, or the leader, must always face the problem of when to invoke the control.

Many groups have formal sanctions that they may invoke against their members. These formal controls automatically call into operation many informal sanctions, both social and internalized. For instance, the placing of a group member on the inactive list may formally restrict him from holding office and participating in certain group functions. It may also informally restrict the amount of association that group members may want to have with him. In addition, other members may set up certain sanctions against him in that they may consider him a "poor group member," one who doesn't take group responsibilities seriously, a person who is not reliable, etc. These informal sanctions give real force to the formal sanction. Controls are most effective when, for a single departure from the existing standards, not one but many separate controls are brought to bear on the individual. When such a complex system of controls is activated, future violations from the group norms are reduced.

The degree of control and the effectiveness of control are related to the importance the group member attaches to being accepted by the group. The identity or "we" feeling the member feels for the group and the relative importance of this group will help determine the effectiveness of the social controls. If there are easy psychological, social, or physical opportunities for group members to withdraw, controls will not be very effective. (The effectiveness of controls upon any member is directly related to the importance assigned by the member to maintaining his membership and status in the group.)

In many cases deviant behavior from group norms may be understood by recognizing that members in a specific group are also members of many other groups that also have standards or norms. Members may not conform to a given group's norms because conforming to the norms of some other reference group is more important to them. For instance, winning may be a vitally important standard to a team group, and this team may place many controls on its members to assure maximum effort toward winning. Some members of the team, however, will not conform to this norm if they must employ unfair tactics to win. Winning by unfair tactics many conflict with standards of other more important groups, perhaps the family or church, and the urge to conform to these standards may be much stronger.

. . . or belong to many groups.

In some cases members may feel they cannot get recognition through the accepted channels of behavior. They may flaunt group standards to get recognition of another kind. A committee member may come to the committee meeting without fulfilling his responsibility of gathering data for presentation and thereby make light of the assignment. (At this stage, the other committee members may convert him to living up to the group standards of a good committee member or invoke additional social pressures upon him to motivate him to live up to the group standard.)

What About YOUR Group?

1. Are group members involved in determining the means — social controls — to enforce group standards?
2. Are the group members aware of the degree of deviation from group standards allowed before social controls are brought into play?
3. Are group standards enforced relatively uniformly — over time and on all members?
4. Are rewards and incentives utilized as means of social control?
5. Are both formal and informal controls and pressures used to maintain group standards?
6. Are there various controls that can be brought into play against deviation from important group standards?
7. Is there a recognition that group members may have group standards of several different groups as their referrants in a given group situation?
8. Are the means of social control reviewed periodically by the group?
9. Is consideration given to making social controls explicit on specific group standards that the group is having difficulty enforcing?

"WE-FEELING" OR IDENTITY

"We-feeling" or identity in a group implies a certain common bond, a common sympathy, and a definite consciousness of being united in some way. This force is sometimes discussed in terms of group solidarity, morale, or *esprit de corps*. The individuals feel a common concern — a stake in what happens to the other members of the group and the group as a whole. The individual feels he belongs, is a part of, and has a common concern with the group. It may be said that these feelings involve the sort of sympathy and mutual identification for which the word "we" is the natural expression.

This "we-feeling" is often manifested by group members when they speak in terms of "we feel," "we believe," "we want," "we demand," "we contend," or speak of "our group," "our problem," and "our achievement." This may be contrasted with other verbalizations such as "they think" or "they do." Usually the pronouns are used as the basis of distinguishing the group to which the individual belongs from some other group — "in-group" versus "out-group."

However, inside any given group there is a wide range of the degree of "we-feeling" or identity with the group. With widely different intensity, members may feel that this is *my* group — "the group whose members I know, whose purposes I share, whose traditions I respect, whose goals I will strive for, and whose prestige I will work to maintain."

Identity is largely emotional, and hence often difficult to account for on any rational grounds. While it may be based on the ideals, philosophy, or objectives of the group, it may be built equally well around feelings toward certain individuals. It may also involve past experiences with the group or perhaps some symbolic meaning which the group conveys to the individual. Any or all of these factors plus many more may be combined in almost any way to produce the feeling of identity between a member and his group.

It is an important point that a member may identify on one basis but not on another. He may identify to a very great degree with the fundamental *purpose* of the group, but poorly indeed with the group itself. He might feel completely at home and happy with the members but have no feeling toward the goals and aspirations of the group. The strongest and most enduring feelings of identity appear to be those founded upon a combination of several bases.

The labor union member may identify with both his union and his company.

People are often identified with several groups. Sometimes either the ends or means of these may be in conflict with each other. For example, a laborer may identify with both his company and his union, even though their interests may clash at times. A business man who identifies with his trade association, his social club, and his church may find that at times his actions in one conflict with the philosophy or ethics of another.

There is a high relationship between identity with a group and participation in that same group and its activities. This is a reciprocal relationship, since greater identification encourages participation and activity within the group is one of the most important sources of identity. Within the group frequent, highly charged interaction — especially under conditions which seem to threaten the group — often leads to exceptionally high identity and solidarity. It has been noted in military organizations especially that *esprit de corps* reaches its peak under conditions of danger or hazard.

Physical conditions which place group members in proximity to each other encourage interaction and hence the feeling of identity. As there is lack of intimacy and greater physical separation, interaction slows down.

The manner in which the ego of the member is rewarded by the group activity has a great deal to do with his ability to identify. It helps if the group goals coincide with his own. It also helps if he feels he has something to say about the operation of the group and the methods it chooses. All the complexities of human behavior enter into identification as it applies to the individual in a group setting.

As pointed out previously, the more group members identify with the group, the greater pressure there is to conform to group standards. Members will be more willing to compromise to secure total agreement. It also seems true that members having a high sense of identity with the group are more willing to sacrifice and work for group goals.

What About YOUR Group?

1. To what degree do the members of your group really identify with the group?
2. Does the group recognize that members may identify with the group in the following ways:
    a. Identity with basic philosophy and purpose of the group?
    b. Identity through common experiences with other members?
    c. Identity with group activities and accomplishments?
    d. Identity with group leaders and other group members?
    e. Identity with symbols that are representative of the group?
3. Is our group providing opportunities and help toward identification?
4. Do members recognize that other group members may identify strongly with other groups?

GENERAL ROLE DEFINITION

The term *general role* is used in this discussion in the sense of the general expectation of the group member's or subgroup's role within the group. In contrast, *interaction roles* will be used in a subsequent section to discuss specific unit acts within the group process. Some expansion may clarify the usage of the term *general role*.

What is the expectation of group members as contrasted with those of the group leader? Is it the group expectation that the leader has major responsibility for group activation, direction, decisions, and action? Or is there a general expectation on the part of all group members that each has a responsibility to help perform all the functions? When a person becomes a member of the group, is he given any definition of his role in terms of the responsibilities, obligations, and privileges that go with the membership? When members are elected to office is there a clear definition of the role they are expected to perform in their given position? Does the *group* know what it expects of its members in general and individual members in particular? On the other hand, do the members or subgroups of members know what is expected of them by the group?

Those organizations which specifically identify the roles of group members are likely to be rated higher in goal achievement than are organizations which do not. If roles are not clearly defined, if there are overlapping roles, or if the defined roles leave responsibility for important functions not specified, there is decreased goal achievement. In addition to decreased goal achievement there are also less favorable attitudes toward the organization and the leadership in the organization. The need for more formal definition increases as the organization becomes larger and contacts are less intimate.

The member's understanding of his role, his perception of how his role relates to other roles in the process of group productivity, and his feeling of the importance of his role all go to determine his sense of responsibility to the group and motivate him to contribute to group productivity. Definitions of roles that evolve from group discussion and participation overtime, or out of election to the role, appear to lead to more productivity than those resulting from assignment or appointment.

If the role of a member is ill-defined and he cannot see how it relates to other roles or contributes to group achievement, he is less likely to be motivated to productive action. The member may not recognize the functions that need be performed or he may be afraid he is usurping the function of someone else. Group member hostility and frustration often results from an unwarranted suspicion of another group member as a threat to his position or as the occupant of a position that is unattainable to him.

But role definitions, as such, do not guarantee group productivity. It should be obvious that roles have real meaning and orientation only when the objectives and standards of operation of the group are clear and common to all members. A lack of clarity or agreement on the ends and the means to attain those ends usually leads to poor definition of roles and lack of motivation for goal fulfillment.

What About YOUR Group?

1. Does your group give attention to the definition of officer, subgroup, and individual member roles?
2. Is there group involvement in the definition of the various group member roles?
3. Do all group members understand how their roles fit into the over-all organizational structure and group goal attainment?
4. Do all group members understand the importance of their roles and how the performance of their roles contributes to group productivity?
5. Are roles defined by default?
6. Are group members left on their own to determine the direction and bounds of their responsibilities?
7. Is there periodic review and evaluation of designated roles?

FUNCTIONAL UNIT ACT ROLES OF GROUP MEMBERS

Many of us have tried to describe what goes on in a group meeting. Some of us have tried to review a meeting to determine why it was a success or failure. Various functional roles of group members are presented here in an attempt to provide a tool that will allow for a systematic recording and analysis of *member unit act roles* in group situations.

It is important to note that we often talk of roles in

terms of the personality type of the individual. There is some relationship between the personality structure of the individual and the unit act roles which members can and do learn to perform. However, most persons *can* learn to perform any of the unit act roles discussed below. The unit act role analyzed here is essentially the minimum recognizable act which fulfills the criteria to be described. So it is quite possible that in expressing one sentence a member may play two or three different roles.

Most of us will not go around with a tape recorder or a chart and attempt to categorize every bit of human interaction we perceive. However, familiarity with the following outline will enable group leaders and members to analyze more or less automatically the unit act roles being played by group members. Many groups and leaders have found the use of this framework has helped them improve their group production. The group member is in a position to play roles needed for group productivity, to encourage others, and to discourage roles that are not contributing to group building or group tasks.

There are two main frames of reference involved in this description.[1] The first involves the mechanism of groups trying to solve problems through discussion and cooperative thinking. A classification of unit acts can be made according to the functional significance of these acts as a part of the problem solving sequence. Broadly these are called *Group task roles.* Any group also has the problem of managing its individual personalities and the emotional and group-oriented relationships. This gives rise to the other significant systems of roles which are treated under the major headings of *Group building and maintenance roles,* and *Individual roles.*

Thus the member roles identified in this analysis are classified into three broad groupings.

---

[1] The basic approach used in this section is taken from Kenneth D. Benne and Paul Sheets, "Functional Roles of Group Members," *Journal of Social Issues,* Vol. IV, No. 2, 1948. With minor modifications the roles and role definitions are theirs.

1. *Group task roles.* Participants' roles here are related to the task which the group is deciding to undertake or has undertaken. The purpose of these roles is to facilitate and coordinate group effort in the definition of a common problem and in the solution of that problem.

2. *Group building and maintenance roles.* The roles in this category are oriented toward the function of the group as a group. They are designed to alter or maintain the group way of working, to strengthen, regulate, and perpetuate the group as a group.

3. *Individual roles.* These are directed toward the satisfaction of the "participant's" *individual* needs. Their purpose is some individual goal which often is not relevant either to the group task or to the functioning of the group as a whole. Such participations are, of course, highly relevant to the problems of group development, maturity, and specific task efficiency.

Group Task Roles

The following analysis assumes that the task of the discussion group is to select, define, and solve common problems. The roles are identified in relation to facilitation and coordination of group problem-solving activities. Each member may, of course, enact more than one role in any given unit of participation and a wide range of roles in the ensuing participation.

THE INITIATOR-CONTRIBUTOR

a. The *initiator-contributor* suggests or proposes to the group new ideas or changed ways of regarding group problems or goals. The proposal may take the form of suggestions of a new group goal or a new definition of the problem. It may take the form of a suggested solution or of some way of handling a difficulty that the group has encountered. Or it may take the form of a proposed new procedure for the group, a new way of organizing the group for the task ahead.

THE INFORMATION SEEKER

b. The *information seeker* asks for clarification of suggestions made in terms of their factual adequacy, for authoritative information, and facts pertinent to the problem being discussed.

c. The *opinion seeker* asks not primarily for the facts of the case but for a clarification of the values pertinent to what the group is undertaking or of values involved in a suggestion made or in alternative suggestions.

THE INFORMATION GIVER

d. The *information giver* offers facts or generalizations which are "authoritative" or relates his own experiences pertinently to the group problem.

 THE OPINION GIVER

e. The *opinion giver* states his belief or opinion pertinently to a suggestion made or to alternative suggestions. The emphasis is on his proposal of what should become the group's view of pertinent values, not primarily upon relevant facts or information.

f. The *elaborator* spells out suggestions in terms of examples or developed meanings, offers a rationale for suggestions previously made, and tries to deduce how any idea or suggestion would work out if adopted by the group.

g. The *summarizer* pulls together ideas, suggestions and comments of group members, and group decisions (decisions of the group) to help determine where the group is in its thinking or action process.

h. The *coordinator-integrator* clarifies the relationships between various ideas and suggestions, tries to extract key pertinent ideas from member contributions and integrate them into a meaningful whole. He also may try to coordinate and integrate the activities of various members or subgroups.

i. The *orienter* defines the position of the group with respect to its goals, points to departures from agreed upon directions or goals, or raises questions about the direction which the group discussion is taking.

j. The *disagreer* takes a different point of view, argues against, implies error in fact or reasoning. He may disagree with opinions, values, sentiments, decisions, or procedure.

k. The *evaluator-critic* subjects the accomplishment of the group to some set of standards of group-functioning in the context of the group task. Thus, he may evaluate or question the "practicality," the "logic," the "facts," or the "procedure" of a suggestion or of some unit of group discussion.

l. The *energizer* prods the group to action or decision, attempts to stimulate the group to "greater" or "higher quality" activity.

m. The *procedural technician* expedites group movement by doing things for the group — performing routine tasks; e.g., distributing materials, manipulating objects, rearranging the seating, running the recording machines, etc.

n. The *recorder* writes down suggestions, group decisions, or the product of discussion. The recorder role is the "group memory."

Group Building and Maintenance Roles

Here the analysis of member-functions is related to those roles which have for their purpose the building of group-centered attitudes and orientation among the members, or the maintenance and perpetuation of such group-centered behavior. A given contribution may involve several roles and a member or the "leader" may perform various roles in successive contribution.

a. The *encourager* praises, agrees with, and accepts the contribution of others. He indicates warmth and solidarity in his attitude toward other group members, offers commendation and praise and in various ways indicates understanding and acceptance of other points of view, ideas and suggestions.

THE HARMONIZER

b. The *harmonizer* mediates the differences between other members, attempts to reconcile disagreements, relieves tension on conflict situations — perhaps through jesting or by pouring oil on the troubled waters.

c. The *compromiser* operates from within a conflict in which ideas or position is involved. He may offer compromise by yielding status, admitting his error, by disciplining himself to maintain group harmony, or by "coming halfway" in moving along with the group.

d. The *gatekeeper and expediter* attempts to keep communication channels open by encouraging the participation of others("we haven't got the ideas of Mr. X yet") or by proposing regulation of the flow of communication ("why don't we limit the length of our contributions so that everyone will have a chance to contribute?")

e. The *standard setter or ego ideal* expresses standards for the group to attempt to achieve in its functioning, or applies standards in evaluating the quality of group processes.

f. The *group observer and commentator* keeps records of various aspects of group process and feeds such data, with proposed interpretations, into the group's evaluation of its own procedures.

THE FOLLOWER

g. The *follower* goes along with the movement of the group, more or less passively accepting the ideas of others, serving as an audience in group discussion and decision.

"Individual" Roles

Attempts by group members to satisfy individual needs which are irrelevant to the group task and which are non-oriented to group building and maintenance point up the need for group and member training. A high incidence of "individual-centered" as opposed to "group-centered" participation in a group always calls for self-examination by the group. The diagnosis may reveal one or several of a number of conditions — low level of skill-training among members, including the group leader; the prevalence of authoritarian and laissez-faire points of view toward group functioning in the group; a low level of group maturity, discipline and morale; inappropriately chosen and inadequately defined group tasks, etc. Whatever the diagnosis, it is in this setting that training needs should be defined. The outright "suppression" of individual roles will deprive the group of data needed for really adequate self-diagnosis and therapy.

THE AGGRESSOR

a. The *aggressor* may work in many ways — deflating the status of others, expressing disapproval of the values, acts, or feelings of others; attacking the group or the problem it is working on; showing envy toward another's contribution by trying to take credit for it, etc.

THE BLOCKER

b. The *blocker* tends to be negativistic and stubbornly resistant, disagreeing and opposing without or beyond reason, and attempting to maintain or re-open an issue after the group has rejected it.

c. The *recognition seeker* works in various ways to call attention to himself, often by boasting, reporting on personal achievements, acting in unusual ways, struggling to prevent his being placed in an "inferior" position, etc.

d. The *self confessor* uses the audience opportunity which the group setting provides to express personal, nongroup oriented "feeling," "insight," "ideology," etc.

THE PLAYBOY

e. The *playboy* makes a display of his lack of involvement in the group's processes. This may take the form of cynicism, nonchalance, horseplay, and other more or less studied forms of inappropriate behavior.

 THE DOMINATOR

f. The *dominator* tries to assert authority or superiority in manipulating the group or certain members. This domination may take the form of flattery, of the assertion of a superior status or right to attention, authoritative behavior, downgrading contributions of others, etc.

g. The *help seeker* attempts to call forth "sympathy" response from other group members or from the whole group, through expressions of insecurity, personal confusion, or depreciation of himself.

SPECIAL INTEREST PLEADER

h. The *special interest pleader* speaks for the "small business man," the "grass roots," the "community," the "housewife," "labor," etc., usually cloaking his own prejudices or biases in the stereotype which best fits his individual need.

What About YOUR Group?

1. Do the group members have an understanding of functional unit act member roles?

2. Have group members developed understandings and skills in role analysis and role playing so that they more or less automatically analyze group discussion as it moves forward and act to see that needed roles are performed?

3. Is the framework of functional unit act roles utilized by the group to analyze and evaluate group process?

4. Do group members often forget about task or group-building roles and center their activity on individually centered roles?
5. Do members become so interested in task roles that they neglect group-building roles?
6. Are members versatile in using the necessary task and group-building roles?
7. Do group members consciously work at expanding their ability to perform needed task or group-building roles?

HUMAN RELATIONS SKILLS

A skill may be thought of as the ability to use one's knowledge effectively. It is a developed or acquired ability. The knowledge referred to in this case is, of course, the knowledge of human relations — working with people and getting along with people. Too often it is assumed that since we have lived all our life with people, we must be proficient in human relations skills. Most of us, for example, have at least the minimum ability to disagree with another without creating open hostility. However, the difference between these socially accepted minimum skills and the skills needed for efficient group member functioning is great.

It is recognized that it is the *individuals* in a group who are the possessors of the human relations skills. Different members in a group possess different levels of understanding and ability in human relations. It should also be obvious that different groups have different average levels of human relations skills. Mature groups, in time, often learn how to work together. They learn what techniques, programs, and divisions of labor work for them as a group and in this sense may be said to have developed a group human relations skill. The degree of such skill possessed by the group may place restrictions on the attainable objectives for the group and the speed with which the group may accomplish those objectives. Of special importance to us in this book is the fact that different levels of human relations skills often place limitations on what techniques may be employed in a given group and on how the techniques that are employed may be used. Thus, the level of human relations skills, actual and potential, is another force that must be taken into account as we work in groups.

For instance, there are certain human relations skills needed to be a good moderator of a panel. First there must be an understanding of what a panel is and what purposes it might serve if used. There must be the skills needed in working with panel members prior to the presentation: to define the problem, set the general limits of discussion, and secure agreement on general procedure. The moderator must quickly define the problem for the audience and set an atmosphere for free and easy exchange of ideas among the panel members. As the panel moves forward, skills are needed to make sure the panel members are communicating with each other and the audience, that the different points of view are being presented, that areas are being summarized and closed off, and new areas opened up. Lack of such a skilled moderator may call for study and training on the part of group members, it may require bringing in someone from outside the group to moderate, or it may necessitate choosing another technique that requires fewer or different human relations skills.

It is accepted that the group has the responsibility of "helping its members grow." In one sense this means that group members must be aware of the level of the human relations skills of the individuals in the group and help them develop understandings and create social situations in which they may develop these necessary human relations skills.

These basic understandings and skills needed for good human relations can be learned and communicated. Studies in industry, the classroom, among voluntary leaders, and in workshops and conferences have demonstrated that these understandings and skills can be communicated to individuals and groups and that their application will lead to higher productivity and morale in groups. It also has been demonstrated that certain limited specific human relations principles and skills can be taught in a relatively short time so that individuals may quickly perform some functions with a relatively high degree of proficiency. The successful training of discussion leaders, recorders, resource people, and observers for specific functions in conferences or workshops has been used to secure this type of evidence.

Leaders who understand and facilitate good human relations in their groups are most successful. Some studies suggest that it is more important for leaders to understand and be skillful in human relations, individual motivation, and group process, than to be *highly* proficient in the subject matter under discussion.

Group member motivation, participation, productivity, and satisfaction are greater when group members possess a relatively high level of human relations skills. There seems to be more group and task oriented activity, rather than personal centered activity when members know and can apply human relations principles.

Industrial studies have shown that from the point of view of both production and worker satisfaction, those supervisors are most successful who give a large proportion of their time to their supervisory function, especially to the interpersonal relations aspect of their jobs. Supervisors in lower producing sections are more likely to spend their time in tasks which men under them should be performing or in the paperwork aspects of their jobs.

It has also been determined that many individuals feel they do not have adequate human relations skills to become members of formal groups. Few people belong to only one organization. They either belong to none (about 40 per cent of the American people) or belong to two or more. Once they cross the threshold and realize they have at least the minimum human relations skills needed, they join several groups. Even among those in groups, one of the important blocks to participation is fear on the part of the individual that he does not have sufficient human relations skills to participate successfully. In some cases this fear and frustration leads to other types of activity — detrimental to group functioning — so that he may get recognition from the group.

Knowledge of human relations is becoming recognized more and more as a science rather than as a group of common sense generalizations. It is also becoming recognized that once people understand the existing principles of human relations they can be taught to apply them with skill rather than learn them in the trial and error method of the past.

What About YOUR Group?

1. Do group members recognize the need for human relations skills for effective group functioning?
2. Does the group accept the responsibility of helping individual group members improve their human relations skills?
3. Do group members and the group as a whole attempt to improve their human relations skills?
4. Does the group actually set up training situations to help group members improve human relations skills?
5. Is the level of human relations skills taken into account in setting group goals and choosing group techniques?

HETEROGENEITY — HOMOGENEITY

The concept of heterogeneity — the presence of differences — is discussed briefly here to help us become conscious that each individual member of the group represents a certain potential in the group. A group must learn to recognize and mobilize all the resources within and without if it is to move toward its goals. If we are to make the most of our potential, we first must know what the potential is. In many cases we have unique member resources that we do not tap because we are not aware that they exist.

The group must serve its members just as the members should serve the group. Specific interests or problems of group members must be known if the group as a unit is to "grow." We often can understand interest, lack of interest, personally centered activity, or aggression if we recognize

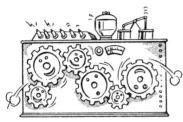

The group must serve the members as well as the members serving the group.

the heterogeneous composition of the group. Group heterogeneity may also place limitations on the objectives, techniques, and accomplishments of the group. The crux is that we must recognize that we have some degree of heterogeneity in all groups and learn to understand these differences from the point of view of how they might be harnessed for greatest group productivity.

We tend to group ourselves on both the informal and formal level on a *relatively* homogeneous basis — a basis of similarities — according to such characteristics as interests, status, intelligence, and occupation. However, even within these relatively homogeneous groups there is a great degree of heterogeneity — differences — when compared on the basis of such characteristics as age, moral standards, formal education, and values. Groups which take the time to analyze their resources from the point of view of both their homogeneity and heterogeneity make better use of their group potential and reach higher productivity. It also seems true that once the group recognizes the uniqueness of individuals they can better integrate those individuals into the group and better utilize their potentials for the common good. Furthermore, group members working together over time tend to become more homogeneous in interests, objectives, and satisfactions.

What About YOUR Group?

1. Do members of the group have different backgrounds, values, interests, abilities, and skills?
2. Are these differences taken into account in group planning?
3. Are relevant differences harnessed and put to work to aid in group progress?
4. Do differences lead to conflict?
5. Is the group becoming so homogeneous that it is over-conservative and tradition-bound?
6. Can new members and different points of view be integrated into the group so as to improve group functioning?

GROUP SIZE

The size of the group is an important force to consider. Much of the research from which the information on group size has been taken has been summarized by A. P. Hare, Laboratory of Social Relations, Harvard University. In many cases little can be done to control the actual number of people in an organization or at a meeting. In other cases, such as committee appointments, control can be exercised.

Size is of particular importance in deciding what group techniques to use under certain conditions to accomplish specific goals. Certain techniques are better suited to smaller groups. Other techniques are better suited for larger groups. Yet other techniques, such as buzz groups, are designed to obtain some of the small group advantages when working with larger groups. Size, like other vectors, has relevance mainly in terms of what the group is trying to accomplish.

Size is one variable that may limit the amount and quality of communication that can take place between individual group members. Thus as size increases, each group member has a more complicated set of social relations to fulfill, and as the number increases, he has proportionally less time to maintain them. There is evidence that an increasing proportions of group members report feelings of threat, frustration, tension, and inhibition to participate as group size increases.

As size increases, there is a greater tendency to move to more formal procedure such as regular parliamentary procedure. With increasing size there seems to be a tendency to strive less for consensus or unanimity. Rather, there seems to be a tendency for the group to reach solutions or decisions without exploring the points of view of all group members, and with less concern for whether or not all group members agree with the solution or decision. Unresolved differences seem to be more acceptable or are at least tolerated in larger groups.

It is generally agreed that increased size is usually accompanied by increased difficulty in coordinating group activities. In larger groups there is a tendency for the formation of small subgroups, often with spokesmen emerging as representatives of the smaller groups. There is evidence to suggest that as groups increase in size, it is more difficult for group members to perceive of other group members as distinct individual entities. Rather they are perceived as members of subgroups or cliques and there is a tendency to deal with them on a nonparticularized basis. Efficient operation in larger groups requires more skill from group members and leaders. However, it does appear that as individuals become more mature, they can more effectively associate in larger groups.

In a study of decision-making groups, with a size range from 4 to 16, the following tentative generalizations were made:

As the size of group is increased from 5 to 12, the degree of member consensus resulting from the discussion decreases when the time for discussion is limited.

Group members in the smaller groups will change their opinions more toward consensus than will those in the groups of 12 or more.

As groups become larger than 12 there seems to be a trend toward factionalism.

. . . there is less concern for whether or not all members agree with the decision

In larger groups the group leaders have less influence and group members feel less satisfied with the discussion because of lack of time to express themselves. Primary groups are more satisfying to group members when they are sufficiently small to give each person a chance to take a full part in the discussion. In the larger group the interaction between members is more limited and the group members tend to have an increasing feeling that their individual opinion is not important and not worth presenting to the group.

Some of the studies in industry have shown that employees in small work groups are more satisfied than those in large work groups. It is doubtful that there is any magic number that is associated with the "best" size group. Efficient sizes may vary with the task, the time available, the maturity of the group, or the amount of follow-up action wanted. However, small group research does have some findings that may have importance in making committee appointments or subdividing larger groups for certain tasks. Small groups (four to six) of even numbers have higher rates of disagreement and antagonism than do groups of odd numbers (three, five, and seven). There is some evidence that discussion groups of five are the best size.

The explanation for five as the "best" size may lie in several factors: (1) this size allows sufficient opportunity for each individual to participate and yet enough members are present to draw on for content and to make it worthwhile; (2) there is not the possibility of a strict deadlock (as with even numbers); (3) if the group splits, it tends to split into a majority of three and minority of two, so that being in the minority does not isolate any one individual; and (4) the group seems large enough for members to shift roles easily and thus any group member may play a role purely for discussion's sake or withdraw from an awkward position.

While most of the evidence cited seems to indicate that increasing size creates problems in group efficiency, this does not lead to the logical conclusion that all groups should be small. From the very practical point of view we know that many formal groups will continue to be large; 20, 50, 100 or more. However, as the sizes of our groups increase, we should be aware of the fact that different degrees of human relations skills are required and we may have to choose different objectives and techniques and be willing to accept different levels of group standards in some cases. As pointed out by Bales, Hare, and Borgatta:[1]

> Many abilities or resources needed in task performance tend to have an additive character. The kinds of resources which are of this order, in respect to tasks, may include such things as the number of items of information which can be absorbed and recalled, the number of critical judgments available to correct errors of information and inference, the number of ideas or suggestions available for solution of problems, the range of values that are likely to be brought to bear, as well as the range of technical skills, abilities, and amount of muscular power that is available to implement decisions.

To this may be added the point that in terms of motivation to action, participation in the decision-making and planning process seems to lead to greater motivation to action and follow-through. Though the larger group involvement

---

[1] R. F. Bales, A. P. Hare, and E. F. Borgatta, *Structure Review of Sociology: Analysis of a Decade*, Wiley, New York, 1957, pp. 391–422.

brings with it some problems in group management, it may well be the most efficient means to accomplish desired action in the long run. In many phases of social action, numbers as such may be an important factor in making a desired impact on other interest groups, community or public — a better government league of 500 "solid citizens" will probably have greater impact on public opinion and action than a committee of five.

What About YOUR Group?

1. Does your group take its size into consideration when planning for group involvement and participation?
2. Does your group utilize group techniques that might aid in getting small group intimacy and personal relations?
3. Is your group large enough that special attention should be given to effective group communications?
4. Is your group large enough that special attention should be given to organizational structure?
5. Is your group of the size that there can be a more or less informal role definition or is it large enough that special attention should be given to more formal role definition?
6. Is your group a worshiper of large numbers? With what size group can the group's purposes really be best served?

GROUP EVALUATION

Evaluation may be a powerful internal force that affects group productivity. We should recognize that evaluation is ever present in groups. In some more or less systematic fashion, consciously or subconsciously, each of us is evaluating our role, status, contribution, or feelings toward the group. We evaluate other group members in the same fashion. We evaluate how well our interests or needs are being met by this group. We evaluate other groups about us. By the same token our group is being evaluated by other groups. Evaluation then is a force that is always present in a group.

The main point to be made in relation to this force is that systematic, rational evaluation has great potential in leading group members and the group to greater productivity. Members participate the most in group activities when they understand the goals and objectives of the group and evaluate the group as making satisfactory progress toward these goals. The more satisfied members are with the progress of the group toward its goals, the more they participate. Those who evaluate the group and its progress and are satisfied with that progress, identify better with the group.

Leaders who make greater use of the various procedures for evaluating their work and the work of the group are more often rated as the most effective. It is even more important in terms of group productivity and morale to know exactly how well the group or individual is doing even when the evaluation is not high. It seems more important to know where you are in terms of progress than to have a hazy idea of where you might be.

It would seem highly desirable for groups to set up some formal mechanism that enables them to evaluate periodically group *process* as well as group *progress*. This enables the group to direct its energies to the specific task at hand, not go off on tangents; to make rational decisions about changes in group goals or process. It affords the possibility of lasting member satisfactions. Specific techniques will be suggested later.

What About YOUR Group?

1. Does the group take time to adequately evaluate progress toward action or content goals?
2. Does the group adequately evaluate group process?
3. Are many group members involved in the evaluation process?
4. Is the group objective about its functioning?
5. Does the group make rational decisions regarding its functioning and does it implement changes suggested?

6. Does the group evaluate accomplishments as well as disappointments?
7. Is evaluation periodic, or is it continuous?
8. Are the results of evaluation available to all members?

*   *   *

Every group has an actual or a potential dynamic state from which will arise the processes and the productivity of the group. Many of the forces which go to establish this dynamism do provide a further step in the development of information which may be applied to all groups — both to encourage their progress and to further their ends.

7.

The External Dynamics of Groups

EXTERNAL FORCES AFFECT all group activities; no group exists in a social vacuum. Such forces as community values, community expectations, institutional values, parent group affiliations and control, intergroup competition, and prestige and status affect every group — its member motivations, goals and means, and ongoing activities. These external forces are reflected largely through the beliefs, feelings, and actions of the members. Examples of how external forces directly affect the actions of *individuals* have already been given. This chapter will treat briefly those broader external dynamics that affect the group as a whole.

Communities are made up of people interacting as individuals and within groups to carry out the activities considered necessary to satisfy their needs. The community develops expectations of various groups, though these expectancies may vary widely from group to group. Certain groups, with certain kinds of members, are expected to perform specific functions for specific categories of people. The freedom with which any group in a community carries on its activities and functions is related to the total community definition of the function and role of that group.

The expectations of a given group may be based upon such things as tradition, past performance, the social status of the membership and leadership, the group's publicly stated purposes, and the public image of the organization and its organizational affiliation. These forces become effective as they are reflected by individual members or by the members communicating and interacting with each other and making decisions.

However, forces may originate from individuals who are not members of the group, from other groups in the community, or from institutions within the community, such as church, school, or business. Or they may come from other groups with which the local groups are affiliated — such as

Certain groups are expected to perform specific functions for specific categories of people.

local Red Cross affiliation with National Red Cross organization. Also forces arise from the more abstract American value system, related to the expectancies of various kinds of groups and group activities.

These external forces may be judged "restrictive" by the group. They may feel certain desired goals and means cannot be adopted by them. On the other hand, the group may judge these external forces as "expansive" in the sense that the group feels the pressure to accept some new and perhaps broader concept of its goals and means. In either case, external forces will affect group functioning.

THE COMMUNITY

Every community has a value system. There is a pattern of acceptable goals and acceptable means for striving toward them. Individuals and groups have status in a community to the extent that they have accepted and achieved (by approved means) the important "community" goals.

Every group has a status in the community, whose members rank it in relationship to coexisting groups. Where and how a group is ranked depends to a degree upon how consistent its goals, objectives, and means are with the general community values. Related to its status is its role — or what the community expects it to do. At any given time two or more groups may be competing for a given status position. Any or all of these forces may affect the goals the group sets, and how it attempts and how hard it will work to accomplish them.

PARENT ORGANIZATIONS

Many local groups have affiliations with an organizational structure which exists outside the community. The Masonic Lodge, the American Legion, the American Red Cross, many church denominations, and Federated Women's Clubs are examples of this type. Most affiliated community groups have a high degree of local autonomy. But there are many instances where the "over-all organization" does exert influence through counsel, guidance, required or recommended programs and policies, and program aids provided to the local affiliate. It is important to recognize that such external forces affecting group *function* exist and must be considered in understanding group *functioning*.

Sometimes groups have problems in this regard because they are affiliated with outside organizations which do not hold the same values as the community. For example, the parent organization may set down certain policy positions on a national level. In some communities these policies may not be completely acceptable. The local unit is faced with the task of adjusting to this difference in values.

Groups, like individuals, can make different adjustments when faced with this kind of a dilemma: they can ignore the community values, which means they risk losing status or being ostracized by the community; they can ignore the institutional values, which means they risk *censure* by the parent institution; or they can try to adjust between the two. The fact that they are an integral part of an extra-community pattern as well as an integral part of the community is a force which constantly influences their activities and behavior. To understand such groups, one must

The local unit is faced with the task of adjusting to the difference in values. . . .

recognize the value orientation of both the community and the parent institutions.

Groups with affiliation outside the community must often walk a tight-wire between individual group member interests, community values, and the values of the "over-all organization." In many cases these are not completely compatible.

Another type of group is found in nearly every community. It is a subdivision of an existing formal structure. A good example is the "ladies aid society" — an integral part of most churches. The goals and objectives of these groups, and their means of attaining them, must be consistent with those of the parent group.

Most communities have groups that are independent of any formal group structure existing beyond the community. This independent group usually reflects community values and the social level of most of its members. Though independent, the community has expectations of the group, assigns it status, and has some influence on it. Such forces will affect its ongoing activities and must be considered in understanding its functioning.

MULTIPLE GROUP MEMBERSHIP

Another pattern of forces at play within each group is created by other affiliations of its individual members. Group members may belong to other groups such as family, church, lodges, friendship groups, clique groups, and unions. An individual's participation in any group is based upon his evaluation of the relative importance of the group's goals and objectives as seen in terms of his personal goals and objectives; i.e., his value system or philosophy of life.

Every individual desires security, recognition, response, and new experience. The relative emphasis he places on these desires is based upon his own experiences which are reflected in his personal value system. The time and energy he gives to any group is relative to his personal evaluation of how much that group satisfies these desires in comparison with other groups of which he is a part or other things which he might do with his time. This is not to imply that this is a calculated rational process for all individuals or that any individual goes through this rational process in all instances.

Time is usually a scarce resource. The degree to which an individual participates in any group depends upon the alternative uses he has for his time. Usually one participates in groups offering the greatest opportunity to maximize the satisfaction of one's basic desires. Desired satisfactions are based upon a personal value system. Thus, the affiliation patterns of group members affect the degree of identity, involvement, and participation in any specific group.

As a result of group participation, individuals become identified in the over-all status pattern of the community. It is a two-way process. Middle-class people tend to associate in middle-class groups; people who associate in middle-class groups become identified as middle-class people; and groups become identified as middle-class because most of their members are middle-class — and so the process evolves.

Groups are usually not completely class bound. They tend to contain a small proportion of members from the class immediately beneath them — often leaders in that class. One way in which an individual moves up the class system is by gaining acceptance in groups which are identified with a class above him. A group may contain members from the social level immediately above its class identity. The research evidence is that few groups include members from more than three strata in their communities.

A group must have social justification in terms of the over-all values of the community if it is to continue to exist and have status. It must have certain goals and objectives related to community goals and objectives. In many cases groups participate in certain kinds of activities to secure this type of social justification from the community. In this sense an external force has affected their group functioning.

UNDERSTANDING EXTERNAL FORCES

Group members wishing to understand the external forces affecting their groups in the total community picture should ask themselves the following questions:

1. How well does this group conform to the community value system, i.e.:
   a. Are its goals and objectives consistent with community goals and objectives?
   b. Do its methods of operation conform to community norms?
   c. How important to the group is this conformity?

2. Does the group have extra-community organizational connections? If so, what is the nature of the extra-community organizational value system? Is it consistent with the community value system and expectations?

3. What are the other associations of the group members?

4. How do the members look upon this group:
   a. How do they define its goals, objectives, and limitations?
   b. How important is the group to them in relation to the other groups of which they are a part?

5. What is the group's status in the community in relation to the other existing groups?

6. What does the community expect of the group:
   a. In terms of goals, objectives, accomplishments, areas of responsibility and activity?
   b. In terms of how the group goes about its tasks?

Answers to these questions should give some insights into the external dynamics that may be affecting group functioning. Also, one can reasonably estimate the community response to any specific action which the group might wish to take.

. . . people who associate in middle-class groups become identified as middle-class people.

CHAPTER

8.

Group Goals and Objectives

"EVERYONE KNOWS why we're here. Let's get on with the job." This is a common enough opening for a meeting. But is it true? Do we really know and agree on what the job is? How will we know we are accomplishing the job? A group unaware of its purposes is a rudderless ship. Cooperatively determined and well-stated goals based on the definite interests and needs of group members will help provide answers to these and many other questions.

According to the analytical framework developed in Chapter 4, all groups have three main areas of interest. They are: (1) the group itself, with its individual members and its internal and external dynamics; (2) the techniques, or means and methods used by the group; and (3) the goals or objectives toward which the group is oriented.

Group goals specify or define its ends; they identify the targets toward which the group activities are aimed. They also provide the framework within which rational decisions can be made about the number and kinds of activities the group should undertake. They should provide criteria against which progress can be measured. When effectively developed and stated they can provide a major basis for common interest, for feelings of identity, for motivation, for group standards, for meaningful participation, and for group member satisfactions.

Our society is replete with groups organized for social action, recreation, self-education, or almost any purpose or combination of purposes. In the midst of all this activity, we should continually ask if important things are getting done. Are these groups really fulfilling the needs of the individual group members, the group as a whole, and the larger society? Failure, in many cases, is not a matter of too few groups, of insufficient members, or lack of effort. More often it is due to failure to analyze important needs in the light of changing conditions, to choose things that are pertinent in terms of the interests and needs of the group or community, and to clearly state realistic objectives that will help meet the needs.

"Everyone knows why we're here. Let's get on with the job."

Most groups have trouble motivating members to participate actively and meaningfully. This problem may often revolve around the lack of clear understanding and agreement on what the purposes of the group are; or around a failure to see how all the activities are really contributing to the attainment of the assumed objectives.

We live in a rapidly changing society. Goals that might have been very important last year may not be important today. The interests and needs of group members change rapidly, indicating the necessity for a periodic review and discussion of group goals and objectives. Such a review may lead to the changing of objectives, a reorientation of emphasis, the adding of additional goals, or even to a recognition of the need for the dissolution of the group. It may also lead to a more specific statement of short-run objectives within the more general framework of existing long-term goals. If study reveals that the objectives of the group should continue as before, it should lead to increased group member motivation based on the reaffirmation of the importance of the group and its goals.

Some organizations seem to exist only because they have always existed and because people keep coming to meetings. Many members do not come, and some who come do not seem highly motivated. A meeting of such a group may appear to be solely for the sake of arranging for more meetings. The objective seems to become that of filling meeting "spots" rather than planning an integrated program that truly contributes to the accomplishment of more important objectives.

We live in a rapidly
changing society.

Sometimes a maze of organization habits — reading minutes, conducting rituals, or carrying out a set order of business — crowd out any important objectives which the group might like to pursue. This can happen to any group. Focusing attention on definite group objectives and on activities designed to help accomplish those objectives will overcome such difficulties.

People continue to participate actively in groups only when it yields certain satisfactions. Satisfactions are based mainly on individual expectations and the fulfillment of those expectations. If there is to be general satisfaction among group members, there must be some agreement on the group's purposes. If members have widely different expectations, it is difficult to see how any specific activities would provide motivation and satisfaction for all. If goals are not clearly defined, it is difficult, if not impossible, to measure progress or accomplishment. The importance of adequately stated goals and objectives in relation to the evaluation process will be discussed in more detail in Chapter 10.

Clearly stated goals and objectives are an absolute necessity for effective decision making regarding activities or techniques which have the greatest potential to aid in effective group functioning and progress.

While clearly stated goals and objectives do not guarantee effective planning, it is difficult, if not impossible, to see how effective planning can be done without them.

GROUP OBJECTIVES AND INDIVIDUAL MOTIVATION

Behind what any member says, behind what he considers important, is his system of values and attitudes.

These values and motivations were discussed in detail in Chapter 5. They vary from person to person. If people are to work together as a group, there must be a certain unity in interests, objectives, and purposes. When people meet and effectively explore their individual interests and

People come with different kinds of expectations as to what the group will do for them.

problems, they soon find it necessary to define their goals and objectives. These will give them a common basis upon which they can work as a group.

Individuals with different expectations, abilities, and backgrounds often have difficulty in becoming a smoothly functioning group. People often join groups with different kinds of expectations as to what the group will do for them. If group members are to enjoy their organization and its functions and gain satisfactions from group participation and accomplishments, they must each feel they have a part in forming its purposes and goals. Each person must feel that the group's goals are consistent with his own, that the group is his group, and that the important decisions of the group are at least partially his decisions.

The basic properties of group goals and individual goals are not fundamentally different. Group activities, like individual activities, are motivated by needs and directed toward goals. Group goals can guide the behavior of group members and motivate them to perform certain activities rather than others. Thus it is important to recognize that group goals can be a source of real influence upon group members.

When a particular group goal has been established, it is expected that "good" group members will work toward its attainment, even when the goal they preferred was not accepted. Individual group members are influenced in varying degrees and in different ways by the various goals of a group. The magnitude of this influence can vary quantitatively among members and from goal to goal for any particular member.

Research tells us that compatibility of individual goals influences the degree to which group goals become established and the amount of influence they will have over members. When all or most of the members of a group have the same goal in mind, it is almost certain that this goal will become a group goal and the group will make a concerted effort to achieve it.

It is evident that group goals must be closely related to the interests and needs of the individual members. The expression of interests and needs by any one member is influenced to a considerable degree by the manifestation of interests and needs by fellow members. This mutual expression and identification of interests and needs is the real basis for the formation of a group and for the formulation of its goals and objectives.

Members who most fully accept group goals display most strongly the drives and motivations which help a group achieve its goals. Those who merely acquiesce are less motivated toward group achievement. Those who reject the group goals tend to pursue individual interests and private goals.

In some groups, members have little knowledge or understanding of group goals. Again, if a group goal is not fully accepted by the members it has little power to motivate the individual toward activities which might lead to its fulfillment. Such a situation is inclined to develop a low level of motivation, rather poor coordination of efforts, and a relatively high incidence of self-oriented rather than group-task oriented behavior on the part of individual members. Member involvement in the process of goal definition enhances the probability that group goals will be understood, accepted, and internalized by group members.

Regular group members influence new members to accept group goals and perform group functions. How effectively this is done depends largely upon the degree to which they satisfy their own interests and needs by participation in the group's activities.

Remember, however, that prospective and new members must have the opportunity to learn about and understand the group's goals. Groups whose members like one another as people, groups that supply personal need satisfactions, and groups with high prestige all exert strong influences upon members to accept their goals.

Many groups have well-defined objectives which give them direction. They have been found to be most productive. Other groups with vague concepts as to why they are organized, what they are attempting to accomplish, or why they are engaged in their activities are less productive. Time spent by group members in effectively defining group goals and objectives can do much to give a group direction and purpose and to increase the quality and efficiency of its achievements.

LONG-TIME AND SHORT-RUN GOALS

Most groups need long-time goals and objectives to give direction to their activities. These goals are often stated at

Time spent by group members defining group goals and objectives can do much to give a group direction and purpose. . . .

a more general level than the short-run objectives. However, within the general framework of the long-time objectives there should be developed intermediate and short-run objectives. For effective program planning it is often important to state the objectives for a specific meeting or even a segment of a meeting. Short-run and intermediate objectives must be consistent with long-time objectives if the latter are to be accomplished, and they should be logically related and integrated to provide for step-by-step progress toward the long-time objectives.

Groups sometimes adopt general, and often abstract, objectives and then proceed to consider them as immediately and easily achievable. Such objectives, especially for groups having relatively infrequent meetings, will usually not supply the needed direction nor allow for a degree of achievement necessary for group motivation, growth, and development. All groups need some short-run, specific objectives that are achievable. A feeling of well-being and satisfaction results from the achievement of any goal. Such objectives help groups to proceed with purpose and in an organized manner; they help insure accomplishment, and permit the identification of evidence for the evaluation of achievement.

LEVELS OF OBJECTIVES

It is also helpful to think of objectives on various levels. Objectives of learning activities in education have been classified into levels and are marked by grade promotion and graduation. In considering objectives for groups and group members, it is helpful to make a similar classification.

Objectives based on the needs and interests of group members as individuals are usually very specific. Examples might include learning to speak more effectively, or increasing understanding of a teen-age son or daughter.

Other objectives may be based on the needs and interests of a group or organization. These are group rather than individually oriented and require the efforts of people working together. Some examples might be to develop favorable public relations with other local service clubs, to secure a new minister, to double the membership of the community club.

Objectives based on the needs and interests of the community, county, state, or nation are dependent upon the joint efforts of *several* groups and organizations. Their objectives might include inaugurating a housing development program for low-income families, bringing about rural and urban understanding of the zoning problems of a growing city, or county school reorganization.

General and remote objectives — the all-inclusive aims of society — are so broad they could serve as an umbrella for most groups and organizations. They might include "strengthening democracy," and insuring the good life for all people.

The needs of individuals and of society must be joined in such a way that both can be met reasonably well. In any group, the *relative importance* and relationship of the *individual member and his objectives* and the *group and its objectives* need to be recognized and understood. One way to visualize this relationship is to consider two circles partially overlapping (Fig. 8.1). One of these can represent the objectives and goals of the individual member of a group (Circle I). The other circle can represent the objectives and goals of the group (Circle G). If these circles overlap, then an individual's objectives and the group's objectives are partially the same (Area C) and partially not the same. The circle representing the goals and objectives of the

. . . to increase understanding of my teen-age daughter.

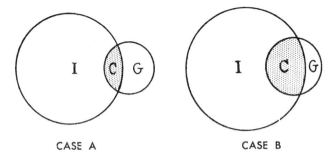

CASE A   CASE B

FIGURE 8.1 — In any group the goals of the individual (I) and the goals of the group (G) overlap (are as marked C).

individual is larger than that representing the group because it is recognized that the interests of an individual member are varied and only a part of them can be met by membership in a single group. Most groups are organized around a relatively few specific interests common to all members.

Individual and group goals and objectives overlap considerably for some members (Case B) and very little for certain members in some groups (Case A). If the overlapping is relatively large, as in B, there should be strong individual member motivation. If this situation exists the groups' chances for goal accomplishment will be improved providing there is appropriate choice of means. This same concept of overlap of group and community goals and objectives is appropriate in any consideration of goals and objectives that are more inclusive than just for any one specific group.

In the actual operation of groups, objectives are a rather complex interwoven network. Sometimes all levels are involved. At times, objectives seem hidden — even lost. Every group periodically needs to review and reidentify its objectives and classify them into their appropriate levels. All objectives must be consistent and compatible at any level just as immediate or short-run goals must be consistent and compatible with intermediate and more ultimate objectives.

STATING OBJECTIVES

Along with an understanding of the levels of objectives, consideration needs to be given to the form and wording of the statement of objectives. A common error is to state as objectives things which people on the various planned programs are going to do for the group. This might be to show how to refinish furniture, to show how to use insulation materials properly, or to present the juvenile delinquency problem. These topic ideas may indicate accurately what the person presenting the program plans to do, but they are not group objectives. Group goals should be statements of what is to be accomplished by or with the group, what is to happen to members of the group, or what the group is expected to do.

The real purpose of a group is not to have certain persons perform activities. It may be to bring about changes in the group and its members, or, if it is an action group, to make group decisions and carry out specified action programs. An objective should identify changes to take place in the group or the kind of action expected of the group and its members.

An objective stated as a planned activity fails to indicate the kind of accomplishment expected. The real purposes of a group are not holding a bake sale or a dance. Instead, such activities are usually a means of accomplishing the group's purposes or objectives. For example, a bake sale is a short-run activity which may raise funds for the intermediate goal of providing a scholarship. This is directed at the ultimate goal of improving the educational level of our citizens. Groups, if they are to be most efficient, must be careful to choose those short-run means-ends complexes (activities) which are not only consistent with, but also positively oriented toward, the intermediate and long-range goals of the group.

Sometimes objectives are stated as general topics or content areas to be handled by the group. Statements of this kind do not specify what is expected of the group. Thus, in a group concerned with health, the objectives might be stated by listing such topics as sanitation, vaccination, or health insurance. A well-stated objective indicates the kind of changes desired in the group and its members, or the action sought. Behavioral changes can be made in group members by changing their knowledge, understandings, skills, interests, appreciations, and attitudes. Objectives of an action group should identify the kind of action expected and the specific end to be accomplished. A group objective is stated with sufficient clarity if a member can describe or illustrate the kind of behavior or action his group is expecting to accomplish.

Another way in which objectives are sometimes stated is in the form of generalized patterns of behavior. Such statements fail to indicate specifically the area of life or the activity to which the behavior is related. For example, one may find objectives that state: "To develop broad interests;" or "To develop desirable social attitudes."

While these indicate the kind of change expected of the group members, it is doubtful if such highly generalized objectives could be very useful to a group. It is necessary to specify more definitely the content area to which this behavior applies, or the situation of the group and its members when such behavior is to be used.

The most useful form for stating objectives is to express them in terms which clearly identify: (1) the people, group, or groups concerned, (2) the kind of behavior or action to be accomplished, and (3) the content or problem area in which this behavior or action is to operate. For example, the following statements of objectives include all three of

. . . to secure a dentist for the town and surrounding community.

these elements. The first is an example of an educational objective, the second an action objective.

People, group, or groups concerned	Behavior or action sought	Content or problem area
1. Members of the homemakers club	To increase knowledge and understanding	About proposed community center
2. Service club sub-committee on health	To secure a dentist	For town and surrounding community

Objectives stated clearly enough to be useful to a group in planning its program and selecting its activities will need to indicate all three of these elements. When objectives are formulated on this three-dimensional basis they become a concise set of specifications to guide the further development of programs and plans. Once goals and objectives are clearly established, alternative techniques or means for accomplishing them can be explored and decided upon and a purposeful plan of action determined.

CRITERIA FOR JUDGING OBJECTIVES

If we hold to the concept that objectives are direction givers, then we must define and analyze them until each word used in stating them helps make them clear and definite. Generalities may create some initial interest, but only specific statements challenge thinking and facilitate planning and action on the part of a group and its members.

Several standards may be used to judge the usefulness of objectives. An organization might judge their objectives by the following questions:

1. Are objectives stated in terms which identify the people or group concerned, the kind of behavior or behavior changes expected of the people involved, and the content or area of life in which this behavior is to operate?
2. Are objectives dynamic — likely to promote action on the part of the group?
3. Are objectives compatible with the general aims of the group or organization?
4. Are objectives achievable considering the level of maturity of the group or organization and permitted by the resources available to the group?
5. Are objectives developmental — will they lead the group to constantly higher levels of achievement?
6. Are objectives varied enough to meet the needs of individuals within the group?
7. Are objectives limited enough in number to avoid undue diffusion of effort within the organization?
8. Can objectives be evaluated — can evidence of actual progress be secured?
9. Were objectives cooperatively determined — was the group as a whole involved in the determination and acceptance of them?

STEPS IN SETTING GOALS AND OBJECTIVES

Groups often fail to take time to define goals and objectives. Resistance is sometimes expressed by such a statement as: "We don't need to waste our time on objectives; let's get on with our work." Another very common feeling is often expressed this way: "Well, everyone knows what we are trying to do."

Sometimes a group can be carried away in their enthusiasm about starting a new project before they clearly think through to their goals. There is only one way to make sure that all members are informed about the group's goals and objectives and that is to provide time to consider them. It is important to allow time for this, especially when a group is just getting organized. When new members are brought into a group, it is important that the goals and objectives be explained to them and perhaps later reviewed and discussed thoroughly.

Another time at which careful restudy of goals and objectives is needed is when a new program is being planned and a new core of officers is assuming responsibility. Whenever a new project or activity is undertaken, it is well to insure that all members are aware of how this new undertaking relates to the objectives of the group or organization.

An important step in setting group goals and objectives is to explore and discuss the members' ideas on what the objectives should be. Allowance should be made for discussing modification and change until the ideas are solidified by the group into definite objectives. To insure acceptance there should be discussion and agreement upon the relative importance of these ideas. After an idea is accepted, it must be put into a meaningful statement.

The last step in setting goals and objectives before securing final group acceptance is checking against the criteria for judging objectives. A short consideration of these criteria will help a group reach right decisions.

Briefly, the steps in setting group goals and objectives are:

1. Provide time for the group to consider them.
2. Explore and discuss the ideas, interests, and needs of the group members.
3. Secure consensus on ideas, interest areas, and needs around which goals and objectives are to be formulated.
4. Formulate statements that explicitly set forth the three necessary dimensions of well-stated goals and objectives.

5. Test each goal and objective against the criteria for judging objectives.
6. Insure common understanding and acceptance by the members of the group.

Once goals and objectives are set, future group experiences tend to be shaped by them and activities can be evaluated in terms of them. The extent that the motivating interests and aims of members of a group are incorporated into its goals and objectives will affect directly the loyalty and participation of its members in the program and activities of the organization.

Sometimes a group can be carried away in their enthusiasm about starting a new project.

9.

Group Techniques

THE MEANS, or methods, used in group situations to bring about group action are called *group techniques*. Regardless of the forces inherent in the group, action comes only through the application of some technique. Utilized in the proper manner and social setting, techniques have the power to activate individual drives and motivations, to stimulate the elements of internal and external dynamics, and to move the group toward its goals.

Schematically represented (as in Chapter 4), the technique is the connecting link between the group and its goals. Better still, techniques — or combinations of them — are the vehicles which carry the group toward its goals. A thorough knowledge and understanding of group methods is a necessary concomitant of good group membership and leadership. The more widespread this knowledge is within the group, the more mature and more efficient is the group. This understanding should be basic rather than superficial and a general discussion should precede any consideration of specific techniques.

It is desirable to re-emphasize that good group techniques are not necessarily formal or organized. Our knowledge of specific methods should not blind us to the fact that *there are always informal techniques at work within any group.* Group process moves by virtue of techniques, however vague, poorly defined, or unrecognized they may be. In small, mature groups with experienced leadership informal methods seem to arise spontaneously and are often the principal techniques used to effect very successful action. Under these circumstances such fluidity of methods may be entirely adequate, but far more often it is necessary to use consciously selected, and often time-tried techniques to "get things moving."

Often it is desirable to set limits on anticipated interaction, or to specify a framework within which such inter-

The group might want to set an atmosphere that would probably produce spontaneity, some freedom from inhibitions, and expression of real emotion. . .

action is to be held. Sometimes it may be useful to set up a social situation in which the type of action and interaction will be fairly predictable. A group might desire to create a certain atmosphere, say of spontaneity and freedom from inhibitions. For these and many other situations there are time-tested techniques; there are also hundreds of other means, formal and informal, which can be used. Creative leadership selects proper techniques, combines techniques, or invents totally new ones to fit situations as needed.

It should again be pointed out that *techniques constitute a means to an end*. Individuals and whole groups occasionally fall into the error of behaving as though their methods were ends in themselves. Situations are created for the sole purpose of demonstrating a facility with a technique.

Ritual, an ancient and still common technique in certain organizations, has often become an end in itself for some individuals. The fallacy of becoming so enamored of one technique that it is used regardless of the situation is also common.

Another error often seen is the use of varied means and methods by leaders who seem to have mastered the application of the methods without understanding their true character or purpose. These leaders have learned that certain techniques work at certain times, but with little idea why.

It should be obvious by this point that while there are many time-tested techniques, good group leadership does not depend upon a "bag of tricks." The whole basic philosophy of this book holds that there are rational processes by which good techniques can be selected and used, but that such use requires basic knowledge, a willingness to diagnose the social situation, and imagination and creativity in the ultimate application.

How then do we make choices and judgments from which good group process derives? It must be done by applying the basic knowledge of all the facets of group behavior discussed up to this point.

SELECTING TECHNIQUES

First, who selects and applies techniques? It might be well to recall Chapter 3 and the discussion of leadership, particularly regarding the opinion that diffusion of leadership represents the most efficient form of the democratic process.

When "leader" or "leadership" is mentioned or implied in the following discussion, remember that the research evidence indicates that the broader the base of such leadership, the more efficient the group is in accomplishing its goals. The authors are also aware from a practical standpoint that ideal situations are seldom achieved and that in many groups the leadership load must be carried by the few.

To return to the outline concept of Chapter 4, the techniques may be considered the link between the group and its objectives. It is therefore logical that in selecting a technique the leaders look both ways; toward the group and its members and toward the ends desired.

First the group — its individual members, its internal and external dynamics — should be considered. The leader must take into account the membership; their interests, drives, and skills as well as their inhibitions, blocks, and frustrations. The human individual is the unit of raw material with which the group leader must work, and the greater the leader's knowledge of human behavior in general and of the individual concerned in particular, the more useful choices he can make.

If a person were in a group largely for the security he felt the group gave him, it might be unwise to place him in a totally new situation. It would probably not be wise to throw one who has great difficulty expressing himself into a situation where he had to give a lecture. Some other technique should be used to tap the resources which this person can contribute to the group. Techniques should be tailored to fit the individuals concerned.

Forces at work within and without the group — dynamics of the group — must be considered in any rational

It would probably be unwise to throw a person who has great difficulty expressing himself into a situation where he would have to give a lecture or a speech.

selection of a group method. Several, or all, of the following elements of group dynamics should enter into the selection of a technique: size, atmosphere, standards, skills available, social controls, identity, general role definition, functional unit act roles, participation, and evaluation.

Group discussion, for example, works best in a small group in which the atmosphere is democratic and permissive rather than tense and inhibited. When a group is large "buzz groups" may accomplish similar ends. This technique is a waste of time when the group is of manageable size.

The most common of all techniques, the lecture, has a serious fault. It is only one-way communication. A very effective method, "role playing," is also dangerous when social controls, identity, and objective evaluation are on an insecure basis within the group. Recreational or musical activities are sometimes chosen to break down status stratification in a group, but if injected into the wrong situation may actually increase hostility and tension.

A full knowledge of the forces making up the internal dynamics is the most likely way of avoiding pitfalls in technique selection.

The leader's choice of a technique will also be affected by what he sees when he looks at the external dynamics. Forces impinging upon the group from the outside may have very significant effects upon the choice of a technique. Some institutions, such as certain churches and schools, frown upon music and dancing, thus placing severe restrictions on recreational methods. Other institutions place certain functionaries above the necessity of answering to the group. It might be unacceptable to involve a member of a church hierarchy in many types of activity, even though it could be very desirable from the standpoint of ends sought.

Community expectations often cause groups to bring in "name" lecturers when a different technique entirely might be more effective. Outside consultants are often used when local people might be expected to do a better job if they were free from community pressures. Choices are affected by the attitude of the community — the external dynamics.

When the method selector looks in the other direction, toward the goals of the group, he will again see a wide and varied assortment of factors influencing his choice. It will be remembered that all goals were divided into those which were strictly informative to the group and those which ostensibly call for action. It is obvious that this division frequently calls for completely different methods. Goals were also divided into long-run and short-run objectives, and again the means of achieving them may be better adapted to one form than another.

. . . or musical games may bring tension, aggression, and disorganization within the group.

If the purpose of a meeting is a straightforward, logical, uninterrupted presentation of a single subject the "symposium" technique might be ideal. If the varying points of view are to be presented by only two people of roughly equal qualifications, the "dialogue" is a useful technique. An interesting combination of several techniques was presented in the Nixon-Kennedy television "debates" in the 1960 presidential campaign. To tap the ideas of as many people as possible, "buzz groups" or "huddle groups" are often used to approximate the benefits of general discussion in small groups. Full group discussion may be the only way to achieve consensus, but to free inhibitions and create a permissive atmosphere it may be necessary to precede this with some recreational or relaxing techniques.

This places limitations on the use of certain techniques.

Another characteristic of group objectives not previously stressed is that almost invariably they are subject to subdivision. Even short-run goals can be broken down into a series of intermediate objectives, and this may also be true of single-meeting goals. Each of the resulting intermediate goals may then be approached with a different technique which would seem to apply more logically to the situation. Combined techniques are really the rule rather than the exception and are particularly used when the objectives can be fragmented.

A general example of this would occur when some group might wish to solve a certain problem — say to improve some item of group process. First, a panel discussion might be set up, with those most concerned presenting the various aspects of the problem. The moderator would have the function of getting the panel under way and of keeping the discussion on the point. An important function of this technique would be to stimulate interest of all participants and to identify essential elements. The panel discussion might end with a general colloquy which in essence would serve to complete the definition of the problem and a crystallization of the essential facts involved. The group might then go into buzz groups to discuss the problem with instructions for each to suggest a solution. Then a general discussion could follow with the aim of achieving consensus. The advantages of such a prepared series of techniques over a desultory general discussion should be obvious as should the fact that combined techniques are often the most effective solution, even to a fairly simple problem.

It should be re-emphasized that to carry out the above program the leadership needs to know much about the individual members and their personalities. Also it is important to understand the "group personality," its internal and external dynamics, and to have a clear appreciation of the specific objectives of the group. An understanding of the basic techniques and what each might be expected to accomplish can then be applied in the selections eventually made.

It is axiomatic in the discussion of methods that each technique has a *definite potential* for the mobilization of individual and group forces and for directing them toward group goals. This potential can only be realized, however, when knowledge, understanding, experience, and skill are present.

Groups are as old as mankind. Some sort of technique for securing group action is certainly as old as communication, no doubt antedating oral language. With the development of languages and written history we find many references to group action techniques in religious, prehistorical, and mythological literature. We recognize the "lecture" technique. Many times we read of groups being swayed to action by forms of the lecture; for example the "harangue" or the "exhortation."

But while group techniques are ancient, their study under scientific methods is relatively new. Revolutions in group methods accompanied the development of spoken language. They were further changed with the advent of printing and the spread of literacy. Today we may be seeing a new revolution centered around mechanical aids: tape, film, television, and amplifiers.

Everything that furthers the group process is a technique. This logically includes coffee breaks, banquets, picnics, and teas. Various types of entertainment serve a similar purpose, and result in group singing, dancing, and talent nights. The difficulty of trying to cover the entire field in detail is apparent.

In Part II, a number of specific group techniques will be discussed in detail. However, those included are rather straightforward, relatively pure types. Social creativity remains the goal of this book, and specific techniques are introduced only to establish a pattern — a study method which will aid the leader as he develops and uses more inventive methods.

10.

Group Productivity, Maturity and Worth

THERE HAS BEEN extensive discussion of the nature, character, and mechanics of the formal democratic group. Many value judgments have been made. It has constantly been assumed that there are poor groups and better groups; that there are useful groups and relatively worthless ones; that groups, like the characters in a TV Western, can be divided into the "good guys" and the "bad guys." It has also been implied that we know the difference. The time has come to consider value judgments, and at least clarify the general opinions as to group quality. This is probably the most difficult segment of the book.

The whole value system of our culture must enter this analysis. We might say that our culture is a synthesis of the Greco-Roman tradition with the Judeo-Christian philosophy, heavily influenced by the Puritan concept of the Reformation and finally distilled out of the ideals of democracy. In other cultures, perhaps where peace and tranquility were the supreme ends, our idea of group worth would be sadly out of place. Our cultural tradition asks that we work hard, that we become productive, that we be self-sacrificing, that the good of the many is more important than the good of the few, and so on.

It is only possible to set up valid considerations as to what makes a group worthwhile under this value system.

We have all heard group members make such comments as: "Our group needs to get better acquainted so that we can cooperate better"; and "There must be more important things on which we could spend our time"; or "Did you understand what we were supposed to accomplish tonight?" Others complain, "Our discussion seems to go in circles, we never decide anything"; while the satisfied comment, "Now that was a good meeting — we got something done."

These and a thousand similar remarks are evidence that group evaluation goes on constantly, and that consciously or unconsciously we all participate. We are interested in the quality of our groups.

The difficulties of communicating the value judgments of our culture regarding the worthiness of groups are largely a problem of semantics. A list of adjectives might be illuminating.

There must be more important things on which
we could spend our time!

Contrast energetic, forceful, experienced, vigorous, useful, stimulating, and dynamic, with lazy, sedentary, dilatory, static, childish, and dull. Adjectives such as these label group activities and our culture has conditioned us to quickly separate the "good guys" from the "bad guys."

Most of us take pride in belonging to groups which get important things done. As members of such groups we are likely to be highly motivated, to participate in depth, and to derive great satisfaction from our membership.

An analysis of these attitudes reveals that group members have two major concerns. What are we doing? And how are we doing?

This can also be stated in relation to the two tasks the group must perform. The *problem-solving and action-accomplishment functions* concern selection, definition, and attainment of goals meeting common needs. The second task, the *process function*, deals with building, maintaining, and strengthening the group structure and activity pattern.

It will be helpful to study the problem-solving function briefly under the term "productivity," and the process function under the term "maturity." The combination of these two, with added considerations apart from them, will make up our final concept of "group worth." Upon this, evaluation must be based.

GROUP PRODUCTIVITY

The idea of group productivity has been discussed in previous chapters. Productivity can be analyzed from several points of view.

One point of view is from that of the group itself. This is probably the most important point of view for this book. Usually we consider a group which effectively selects realistic goals and effectively and efficiently accomplishes those goals as a productive group. However, the acceptance of the importance of the democratic philosophy and process in voluntary groups may impose several additional qualifications on our judgment as to whether a group is productive.

The over-all evaluation of the relative productivity of groups is often colored by judgments about the "costs" of such productivity. In democratic groups there is the concern for the dignity of the individual, his rights, interests, needs, and development. Thus, the judgment about productivity in terms of the accomplishment of goals is usually made by taking into consideration the use of acceptable means.

Productivity can also be analyzed from the point of view of the community or larger society. From the community or larger society standpoint, that group which promotes and accomplishes the most for the general good may be considered most productive. However, the authors prefer to discuss this aspect of productivity from the point of view of the *worth* of the group. This discussion is reserved for a later part of this chapter.

GROUP MATURITY

In contrast to group productivity (which was discussed as representing the problem-solving function of the group), maturity is used here to represent the process function. While not a perfect synonym, it satisfactorily symbolizes the characteristics involved.

Ordinarily, the mature group will be effective in the process function; but it is well to remember that it should also be the most productive. Effective organizations in the problem-solving area usually behave in such a way as to insure great motivation, individual satisfactions, and high group morale. Before these can be attained it is usually necessary to reach a high degree of *maturity*.

The length of time the group has existed or the number of times it has met are not very good criteria of maturity. We all know individuals of mature chronological age who are still immature, and so it may be with groups. The assumption is that maturity connotes certain qualities of experience and "know how," without loss of youthful vigor and drive. Immaturity connotes lack of "know how," as well as a certain instability associated with extreme youth. It has proven useful to develop a set of objective criteria as a frame of reference for judging group maturity.

Maturity in an organization does not spring up spontaneously. It is developed by sound practices and by skilled and artful leadership. How can this be encouraged?

Every individual, and every aggregate of individuals, has unique attributes and characteristics. Methods helpful in one instance may prove useless in another. It is important that creative efforts be expended in the direction of maturity; no simple formula for action will do.

The more specific characteristics of mature groups have been assembled to help in this project. They can enable us to look objectively at group functioning and to have a more precise orientation toward maturity.

Group maturity is most evident through the harnessing of group member skills and combining them effectively. Immature groups become mature by this process. At the same time, unproductive groups become productive. It is quite possible that group processes developed for one stage of maturity will have to be altered as conditions change, as new problems present themselves, or as greater maturity is achieved. A group unwilling to change its pattern of operation, no matter how effective it has been in the past, may have passed through maturity and be approaching senility. If the group is to remain vigorous, there must be constant analysis and adjustment. In some cases a mature group may even decide to terminate its existence if a need for it is no longer recognized.

A group may decide to terminate its existence.

CRITERIA FOR A MATURE, PRODUCTIVE DEMOCRATIC GROUP

According to Haiman,[1] a mature, productive group is, in broad general terms, one which, within the framework of democratic values, makes progress toward its goals with a maximum of efficiency and a minimum of wasted time and effort. This would seem to lean more toward the definition of productivity than toward that of maturity. Another definition describes the mature group as a self-directing, self-controlled body in which every member carries his part of the responsibilities for developing and executing the group's plans.[2]

The following list of criteria for the mature group (adapted from Haiman) is presented as a general outline for stimulatory thinking and discussion. This will enable the reader to better identify the specific elements pertinent to any special situation. These criteria can be used by any group as a framework within which to analyze and discuss its own qualities of maturity. Such study should lead to better insights into group strengths and weaknesses.

A mature group is one which:

1. Recognizes the values and limitations of the democratic procedures.
2. Provides an atmosphere of psychological freedom for the expression of all feelings and points of view.
3. Achieves a high degree of effective intercommunication.
4. Has a clear understanding of its purposes and goals.
5. Is able to initiate and carry on effective, logical problem solving which results in action.
6. Recognizes that means must be consistent with ends.
7. Faces reality and works on a basis of fact rather than fancy.

---

[1] F. S. Haiman, *Group Leadership and Democratic Action*, Houghton Mifflin Co., Boston, 1951, pp. 103–4.

[2] D. M. Hall, *The Dynamics of Group Discussion*, The Interstate, Danville, Ill., 1950, p. 3.

8. Provides for the diffusion and sharing of the responsibilities of leadership.

9. Makes intelligent use of the differing abilities of its membership, and recognizes the need for and utilizes outside resources.

10. Strikes an appropriate balance between group productivity and the satisfaction of other felt needs.

11. Provides for satisfactory integration of individual values, needs, and goals with those of the group.

12. Is objective about its own functioning; can face its procedural-emotional problems and can make whatever modifications are needed.

13. Has the ability to detect rhythms of fatigue, tension, emotional atmosphere, etc., and to take measures for their control.

14. Achieves an appropriate balance between problem solving and process orientation.

15. Strikes a useful balance between using established methods and a willingness to change procedural patterns to meet a situation.

16. Has a high degree of solidarity, but not to the extent of stifling individuality.

17. Finds a healthy balance between cooperative and competitive behavior among its members.

18. Strikes a balance between emotionality and rationality.

The specific subject of group maturity should not be dismissed without some discussion of the immature group. This is often a newly-formed group. It may be awkward and uncoordinated in its behavior. The structure of organization and communication is often frail. In such a group, normally well-adjusted persons may develop insecurity. This may be due to lack of clarity regarding goal orientation, role expectations, communication channels, or acceptable standards of performance. Unclear status relationships within the group may lead to insecurity. Under these conditions one might expect a low level of individual identity and poor group cohesion leading to lack of participation, to

A newly-formed group may be awkward
and uncoordinated in its behavior . . .

a high incidence of personally centered roles being played, or to a high degree of emotional rather than rational behavior.

Building group maturity calls for renewed attention to goal definition, role definition, standards, and choice of techniques. Opportunities must be created for individual satisfactions and hence to increased identification and group cohesion. Individuals must be reassured and supported in their roles and provision must be made for the realization and expression of personal satisfactions resulting from the attainment of short-run objectives.

GROUP WORTH

In the process of group participation, an individual may become so involved in the sheer satisfactions that he gets from being a part of his groups that being objective and analytical about them is pushed into the background.

So far, the authors have discussed groups with the intent of helping individuals make their groups better. This approach ignores an essential aspect of group participation which every individual, because of limited time and resources, should consider. This is the intrinsic and societal worth of the various groups to which he gives time and energy.

In a democracy, the authors fully recognize that each individual has the right to choose the groups of which he wishes to be a part. As was pointed out earlier, there are many different reasons for a person's belonging to any given group. In most instances, these reasons can be subsumed under the rubric of individual maximization of personal satisfactions. In approaching the choice of one's groups from this short range point of view, an important aspect of democratic groups is liable to be ignored. Democracy allows everyone the freedom to choose, but with democratic freedom always goes the responsibility of making choices which tend to perpetuate the system which allows this basic freedom. If the system is not perpetuated, the freedom to choose is lost. The concept which places the individual above the state and guarantees his right to his individualism can be lost to the opponents of this concept of individual rights; totalitarian philosophies nurtured by elements of the Extreme Right or the Extreme Left. Neglect, resulting primarily from the lack of concern on the part of those who take the democratic system for granted, provides the arena in which these forces operate.

By its very nature, a democratic society places a dual responsibility upon the individual. He must accept the responsibility of choosing and performing a useful function which provides him with a modicum of economic returns and he must take an active role in maintaining the system which allows him the right to make choices and maintains him as an entity which is more important than the state.

If one accepts these assumptions, then one must choose to participate in some groups which contribute to society as a whole.

A member of a democratic society occasionally needs to take inventory of the groups in which he participates to determine how many of them are taking his time and are really not making much of a contribution to his long range goals even though they may be providing him with short run satisfactions.

In a democratic society, many groups are perpetuated

long after the purposes for which they were established have been fulfilled. These groups continue as honorifics who meet for meeting's sake.

Groups which establish arrival dates of one's ancestors are unique to societies such as the United States which have been established by large scale immigrations. Having ancestors who arrived early gives status to individuals in all relatively new societies even though this concept is anti-democratic. In every community throughout the land, there are groups whose sole purpose is to establish that certain members of the community had ancestors who arrived early in the settlement of the country. These groups occasionally take on worthwhile tasks to justify their existence, but their real purpose is to provide status for those who are ancestrally qualified.

There are many groups whose sole function is to provide a communications situation in which local gossip is exchanged and social controls brought to bear in the community.

The authors are not contending that individuals should refrain from participating in the above mentioned types of groups. They are contending that such groups are of auxiliary worth to a democratic society and that the individual, while he has the freedom to choose any group he wishes, also has the responsibility to perpetuate the system which provides such freedom. Thus, the individual should evaluate the worth of the groups in which he participates from two, not necessarily conflicting, points of view: his own satisfactions and the actual or potential contribution these groups make to other group members and the larger society. Since most individuals do not have unlimited resources to allocate to group activity, a conscious rational evaluation may lead to a reallocation of resources to other more significant groups.

11.

Group Evaluation

EVEN A SUPERFICIAL CONSIDERATION of the tremendous number of man-hours expended upon group effort inevitably raises the question: "Is all this worthwhile?"

In a specific group, this often takes the form of frustration, disinterest, or apathy, perhaps expressed as: "We just aren't getting anywhere." Members are often unable to identify the sources of these feelings and lack the necessary skills to diagnose and correct the basic causes. Failure to achieve group goals or to make satisfactory progress toward them usually lies at the heart of such dissatisfactions.

The process of assessing the degree to which a group is achieving its goals constitutes the heart of evaluation. Every group needs to use evaluation in order that it may be as productive as possible.

It has been suggested that random evaluation is always present in any group situation; its usefulness, however, is strictly limited. It may have an effect, but often due to the

Evaluation has been going on constantly in all groups.

pithiness with which it is expressed or to the status of the critic rather than to its pertinent constructive qualities.

Not all random evaluation comes from within the group. The community in which a group functions also considers it a prerogative to comment upon the group's actions. "They're just a bunch of snobs," "a mutual admiration society," or "they really get things done," are comments representing unorganized external evaluation. Derogatory remarks are more likely to be voiced than commendatory, but even these often indicate the high regard in which the group is held. The truth or falsity of such remarks usually cannot be substantiated, but taken together they help make up the public image of the group and contribute to its dynamics.

Who should evaluate a group? It might be considered that external evaluation would be more objective than internal and hence more useful. The flaw in this view lies in the fact that only the members can be fully aware of all the nuances of their process. Under the democratic concept the members themselves are chiefly involved in goal setting and only they can sense all the ramifications, even when well verbalized. Only the members can estimate the satisfactions they are receiving from participation. Hence, in the context of this study of the group in action, the members themselves are the best qualified evaluators.

One important exception should be noted. Certain groups are subsidiary to a larger organization. In many cases the parent group retains the privilege, in varying degree, of periodically evaluating the process of the local unit. Organized evaluation of daughter organizations by outsiders representing a hierarchy or bureaucracy may have excellent justification. It remains, however, peripheral to the primary focus of this book.

Evaluation is a difficult process. It deals with people, and human behavior is always complex. There is usually resistance to evaluation, since the members, both individually and collectively, are inclined to fear and resent it. Groups as well as individuals have difficulty viewing themselves without bias and any attempt at examination or criticism is apt to provoke resentment. They may fear the results or doubt their value. Some have had unhappy experiences with poorly conceived evaluations and have developed a defensive attitude. One of the important tasks of good leadership is that of educating the membership to the necessity for evaluation. Rational approaches to the problem can do much to break down the emotional resistance.

Another obstacle to effective evaluation is the difficulty in establishing standards upon which judgments are to be based. In the long continuum from uselessness to perfection, "good" and "bad" must of necessity be arbitrary stops selected by the group itself. Education in this regard is a part of the approach to evaluation. Such judgments as to what the group expects of itself should be demanding, but realistic, if they are to be of maximum value.

A third deterrent to useful evaluation has long been a lack of suitable instruments of precision for carrying it

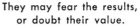

They may fear the results, or doubt their value.

out. Many devices have been constructed and used; some have been faulty, and nearly all have been subject to misunderstanding and misuse. Improvement in this regard is discernible, however, and the pattern of this progress will be developed later.

If, as has been pointed out, evaluation is always present, the challenge is to improve its quality. Random evaluation tends to be subjective, unsystematic, and superficial. Such disorganization is often more destructive than useful. The manifest evils resulting may largely be prevented in good evaluation by (1) making sure it is objective in character, and (2) making sure it is meaningfully structured rather than unstructured.

Always remember that evaluation is a means to an end. Its prime purpose is to indicate changes for the future which will increase group productivity, maturity, and worth. It might also be described as a comparison of the actual with the ideal, to the end that judgments of progress may be made. It is an essential ingredient of group process, and intelligently and skillfully used may become a vital force in its improvement.

Good evaluation demands a great deal of a group and of its leadership. Knowledge of the various forces making up the dynamics of group action is essential to the selection of suitable techniques. Such knowledge also makes a group receptive to evaluation and capable of making use of the facts elicited by it.

In the attempt to bring meaningful structure to the problem of evaluation, the first question to be answered is: What are we evaluating? All aspects of group activity may call for evaluation; both the goal-attainment function and the process function need inspection. It is obviously unrealistic to attempt to make judgments over such a broad and diffuse range at any one time. It is necessary to choose some facet of group process upon which the interest of the group can be focussed and for which the need can be demonstrated. There must be a clear definition of the purpose of any evaluation before a technique can be chosen, or a new one designed. With this accomplished it becomes feasible to talk about means.

The following outline should facilitate referral to some of the elements of group functioning which can be evaluated.

A. The group and its dynamics
1. Atmosphere or climate of the group.
2. Communication pattern of the group.
3. Involvement, or participation pattern of the group.
4. Level of performance as compared to standards.
5. Degree of social conformity; social control.
6. Degree of identification of members.
7. General role definition of members and subgroups.
8. Unit act roles performed by members.
9. Individual human relations skills.
10. Quality of the resolution of individual differences.
11. Adaptation to group size.
12. Use made of evaluation.
13. Conformity to community values and goals.
14. Status of the group as related to others.
15. Community expectations and group goals.
16. Identity with institutional values.
17. How extra-community controls affect the group.

B. Goals and objectives
1. Effectiveness of goal consideration.
2. Degree of consensus in objective formulation.
3. Understanding and acceptance of goals.
4. Clarity of the statement of objectives.
5. The dynamic qualities of group goals.
6. The achieveability of objectives.
7. Compatibility of goals with community values..
8. The developmental aspects of goals.
9. Cooperative determination of goals.
10. Evaluation potential of goals.

C. Techniques
   1. Appropriateness in relation to member abilities and skills.
   2. Appropriateness in relation to internal dynamics.
   3. Appropriateness in relation to external dynamics.
   4. Compatibility with stated objectives.
   5. Creativity as expressed by adaptation and invention.

Once a group obtains consensus on the need for evaluation and on an area suitable for its application, methods for carrying it out must be chosen. Evaluation methods are simply group techniques. They occupy a position in group process comparable to organization techniques, planning techniques, information techniques, or action techniques. Actually, many techniques originally developed for entirely different purposes may be applied as evaluation methods. For example, small group discussion, panel discussion, and many others may be used primarily for evaluation if properly structured. Many methods have also been designed specifically to accomplish objective and meaningful evaluation.

Specific evaluation techniques may best be illustrated by the use of check lists developed to facilitate the application. These forms are only tools for the accomplishment of the technique and should not be regarded as the complete description of the method. A number of examples of these forms are exhibited in Part II to help illustrate the various types and levels of evaluation. Each has been designed and used for a specific purpose and will probably not serve in another situation. It should prove useful to study them, and the rationale behind them, prior to adapting them and creating new techniques to meet the special needs of the individual group.

Pending the presentation of the more detailed technical devices in Part II the following discussion may be considered introductory and for orientation only.

The most elementary technique for evaluation is simply heeding the unstructured random criticisms which occur constantly. A first step in formalization would be to request comments from the membership from time to time on specific items of group progress and process. It is quite a common practice to pass out "end-of-meeting" slips asking for written comments which can then be discussed. This is further elaborated under evaluation techniques in Part II. Such simple methods have their value. A collection of such comments, with or without signatures, produces many worthwhile ideas and has the great advantage of giving everyone an opportunity to participate. If such slips can be collected and summarized by really objective members, and if this is followed by intelligent discussion, much benefit may ensue. Often, in a group not accustomed to evaluation and not completely sold on it, this may be the most that can be attempted. It falls far short of the ideal, however.

More sophisticated and meaningful methods which involve the entire group can only be developed and applied as the group begins to see the value to be derived and to overcome their fears as to the results. The development of better methods of whole-group evaluation, of which there are many, calls for a re-examination of the basic elements of group process, particularly its internal dynamics. Forms based upon internal dynamics of a group and upon the concept of group maturity will be presented. Progress toward goals was mentioned as an extremely important as-

"End-of-meeting" slips should be collected and summarized by really objective group members.

pect of evaluation, and a device designed to measure this is also given among the whole-group evaluation forms.

The evaluation techniques suggested so far involve the entire group in the procedure, usually by filling in forms or check lists. An alternative method consists of the use of a group observer, or an observer team. This may involve the use of personnel outside the membership, but usually and more usefully makes use of artificially externalized group members who are assigned the responsibility for observing and reporting on the interaction and process of the group. The importance of having individuals of the highest possible ability in human relations skills for this post should be obvious. They must have the basic attributes of tact, politeness, and diplomacy as well as an extensive knowledge of group dynamics if they are to observe and report objectively as a basis for evaluation.

Two principal forms of observer function are noted. The anecdotal observer concentrates upon the group as a whole — how it functions, what difficulties it encounters, and how these might be overcome. The verbal interaction process observer focusses attention on the individual participation of the group membership. The pattern of interaction and the qualitative aspects of participation may be determined and recorded, often diagrammatically, by some of the devices which have been developed in this field. By determining the unit act roles (described in Chapter 5) played by the individual members and by recording the

Another way to make these kinds of evaluations is to record who participates and the purpose or unit act role performed. . . .

number of times specific roles are played and the sequence in which they appear, the observer may shed much light on the real causes of group success or failure.

Group observer devices may attain a considerable degree of complexity. Advanced methods attempt to record interaction on both a quantitative and qualitative basis. In addition to recording the nature of participation, these methods try to record the direction and the vigor or force. This can be done verbally, but it is more common to resort to graphic methods. The resulting diagram is known as a sociogram. This technique calls for highly skilled observer teams, and it also is axiomatic that small segments of group process, both in content and time, must be selected for such study in depth.

Along with the forms and check lists for gathering evaluation material shown in Part II will be found some descriptive material and some actual illustrations. Groups should, however, develop and use their own evaluation tools according to their particular needs. Any attempt to fit the group's problems to the specific examples cited can only limit creativity and ultimately down-grade the quality of the evaluation.

Evaluation seems very prone to slip away from the mainstream of group process. With some it becomes an end in itself, rather than a means to group improvement. To others it turns into a pleasant pastime which always amuses but never arouses the membership. Improperly managed, evaluation can be a destructive force, demolishing group unity and undermining established and effective procedures of all kinds. It calls for highly developed skills in its institution, its use, and in its final interpretation and implementation.

The discussion may have inadvertently left the impression that gathering material for evaluation *is* evaluation. Information assembled by any means is only the raw material for evaluation. It must be summarized and reported to the group, and only the group consensus can establish the interpretation to be put upon it and decide what action is to ensue.

If evaluation has been well conceived the entire group will understand its purposes and the implications of the data obtained. One of the chief benefits of evaluation lies in its educational aspects. There is no better way to learn the elements of group process than to apply them in an evaluation analysis. The manner in which group members can bring maturity and objectivity to the interpretation and application of evaluation data is a measure of their understanding of the group process as a whole.

Evaluation need not be complex or difficult. Quite often the most simple form that can be devised will be the best. Evaluation cannot be imposed upon a group which does not wish it, but some form of structured evaluation will be of benefit to any group. Selling, explaining, and teaching evaluation is a function of the leadership, but the practice and interpretation is a matter for the whole group. One of the goals of the study of groups is to improve group productivity. Evaluation is a potent force toward this goal.

Evaluation demands a great deal of leadership.

PART

2. Techniques

Introduction

MOST PEOPLE HAVE "how to" questions about the group process. They want to know how to improve groups, how to develop leadership, and how to secure group action. These have been their aims in reading this book. It has been consistently maintained that only by a basic understanding of the socio-psychological and sociological factors involved could these questions be answered and those answers put to use. While this section will approach the question of techniques in a "how to" fashion, no dilution of this principle is implied. Without the basic philosophic discussion and the general system of analysis of group process which has been given, the subsequent material would not be very meaningful.

Techniques have been likened to the vehicle which helps move a group toward its goals. The specific, representative, methods which will be presented in considerable detail are merely examples of some of the most familiar of these vehicles. Some are common, and have simply been analyzed by modern sociology for better description. Others represent modern revision, expansion, or invention, developed as better understanding of the nature and importance of group techniques has appeared.

The specific methods presented fall rather naturally into three groups. The first group might be considered "meeting," or "session" techniques, designed to either bring information and understanding to a group, or to move a group to action. Examples of this technique will be presented in considerable detail. Techniques to be used when the group situation is expanded, either in size or in time, are dealt with in considerably less detail in the second instance. Evaluation methods, essentially a technique for improving group process rather than for approaching specific goals, make up the third set of methods to be presented.

The choice of the specific techniques to be described under the first category carries no implication that these are the best methods. All are designed, ordinarily speaking, to inform or to stimulate action and are basically applicable to the single session, or even only part of a session. They are presented in the main in a "pure" form with complete realization that they are seldom, if ever, put to use in exactly the way described. There are three reasons why it is important to understand these pure forms as they have been analyzed and recorded by students of group process.

1. There is considerable confusion as to the nature of many of the techniques. For example a panel discussion may be condemned as unsatisfactory for a certain purpose after a demonstration which was *called* a panel discussion, when the whole process was in fact a symposium. Therefore the more or less well known methods should be carefully defined.

2. Many of the most successful group methods are achieved by combining techniques, and an intelligent combination depends first upon understanding the elements to be combined.

3. A description of a number of the best known and most frequently used techniques in "pure" form allows for the development of an outline format, a logical framework which anyone may find valuable in devising new techniques.

The format under which each of the well known techniques is presented constitutes a framework for its application. It consists of an opening statement containing a definition of the method and noting the important elements of internal dynamics which it brings to bear on the problem at hand. The potential forces available in the technique are summarized. The essential purposes or objectives for which the technique might be chosen are then considered. This is followed by a listing of the usual conditions under which, or situations in which, it may be useful. A check list of the steps in the application is then given, both from a general standpoint and from the standpoint of all the usual leaders involved. In essence the questions "why," "when," and "how" regarding the method are answered. A final section of cautions or warnings about some of the hazards of the techniques ends the presentation.

In spite of the fact that only generally applicable ma-

A panel may be condemned because there has been no interchange of ideas between panel members.

terial can be used in these outlines, they reach a rather formidable length. The reader may wish to read only the opening discussion of each and the full outline in a few cases. Experiences have shown, however, that when someone actually starts to apply an unfamiliar technique there is almost never enough detail available to satisfy his desires. Hence the rather extensive and detailed presentation.

Many group situations are either too large or too long lived for any single technique to be generally applicable. Therefore, in a much less detailed manner, some attention is given to working with large groups, to conferences, workshops, institutes, and the like.

Evaluation techniques, making up the third grouping, are presented in another manner. Essentially these are group process techniques and their first reason for existing is to improve the workings of the group. In a secondary fashion, however, they may be among the most valuable ways of eventually achieving both group education and group action. There is some discussion of the various ways of going at the type of group introspection called evaluation and these ways are illustrated chiefly by the presentation of forms on which evaluation may be recorded. Again, they are only illustrative, and methods designed on the spot to fit individual situations will usually be much better. Considerable knowledge of group process and a knowledge of how others have gone at the job will contribute immensely to the creation of evaluation techniques.

Finally it is hoped by this approach to develop skill in selecting a technique, in applying it, in the combining of techniques, and most important of all, in creating technical solutions to problems as they arise.

1.

Small Group Discussions

THIS TECHNIQUE may be defined as face-to-face mutual interchange of ideas and opinions between members of a relatively small group (usually five to twenty). It is more than the random, desultory, or unstructured conversation which occurs whenever small groups congregate; it has method and structure, but it can still be informal and democratic in every sense. The occurrence of a small group discussion implies a common concern regarding a desire for information, a problem to be solved, or a decision to be made.

DYNAMIC CHARACTERISTICS OF THIS METHOD

1. It permits maximum interaction and interstimulation between members.
2. It can place responsibility on all members to participate and to be prepared with facts and ideas.

3. It can teach members to think as a group and develop a sense of equality.
4. It sets up situations from which leadership may emerge.
5. By it all members may broaden their viewpoints, gain understanding, and crystallize their thinking.
6. By it members are encouraged to listen carefully, to reason, to reflect, to participate and to contribute.
7. It permits leadership responsibility to be shared by all who contribute.

THIS METHOD MIGHT BE CHOSEN . . .

1. To identify and/or explore mutual concerns, issues, or problems.
2. To increase awareness, appreciation, and understanding of mutual concerns, issues, or problems.
3. To generate interest in ideas, issues, and problems.
4. To supply and diffuse information and knowledge.
5. To motivate a group to action.
6. To involve members in the problem-solving process.
7. To get members to crystallize their own thinking.
8. To form group opinion or concensus.
9. To assist members to express their ideas in a group.
10. To create awareness of issues and problems.
11. To encourage and stimulate members to learn more about problems and ideas.
12. To develop a core group of people for leadership purposes.
13. To develop an informal and permissive group atmosphere.

THIS METHOD IS USEFUL . . .

1. When the group is small enough for everyone to be involved in discussion.
2. When the members have enough interest in the prob-

lem and want to know more about it or solve it through overt participation.

3. When the group members are willing to listen to all sides of a problem and work for agreement, understanding, and/or solution.

4. When the group standards are such that members of the group are willing to exchange ideas and points of view and to explore deeply into a problem.

5. When there is a willingness and skill on the part of the members to communicate with each other.

6. When the level of human relation skills of members is adequate to facilitate good discussion.

7. When there is enough difference or heterogeneity of opinion and understanding to make discussion productive.

8. When the group atmosphere is such that permissiveness and good feeling prevails.

9. When the participation is to be distributed throughout the group and not leader centered.

10. When there is need for some members to strengthen their identity with the group.

11. When members have some understanding of functional unit act roles.

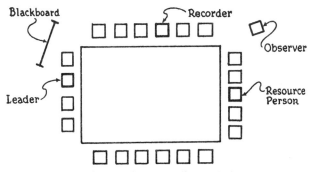

A suggested setup for a small group discussion.

HOW TO USE THIS METHOD
The Group Should:

1. Have the group objective clearly in mind and the meeting, or segment of a meeting, in which the technique is to be used.
2. Consider alternative means that might be used to accomplish the objective.
3. Make sure the group has a problem, idea, concern, or issue that is worthy of discussion.
4. Select or provide for the selection of a chairman who can think rapidly and clearly, who can ask pertinent questions and not take sides, who can stimulate thinking, and who can summarize well.
5. Select a meeting place appropriate to the size of the group.
6. Arrange the group in a circle or square so each person can see every other person.
7. Provide table space if convenient for the entire group.
8. Keep it informal by having all members, including the leader, stay seated during the discussion.
9. Have proper equipment, such as blackboard, chalk, and paper, available.
10. Appoint a discussion recorder.
11. Give everyone a chance to talk but agree there will be no "speech-making."
12. Encourage ease, informality, good humor, and friendly disagreement.
13. Keep the discussion directed and on the track — but let the group lay its own track.

Give everybody a chance to talk, but don't tolerate "speech-making."

14. Take time at appropriate intervals, at least every 10 or 15 minutes, to summarize and draw loose ends together.
15. Keep the group conscious of accomplishment and of the objective by frequent statements of progress by the chairman and/or recorder.
16. Discuss with fairness and objectivity, and avoid fault-finding, bias, and cynicism.

The Group Leader Should:

1. Meet with other members of the leadership team and discuss the functions and operations of the team.
2. Assist the group to define clearly their problem or objective.
3. Aid the group in establishing the necessary structure to accomplish their objective.
4. Encourage the expression of ideas by all members of the group.
5. Refer questions back to the group.
6. See that facts are made available when needed.
7. Ask questions and make summaries without letting personal views intrude.
8. See that all aspects of the question or problem under discussion are explored.
9. Help the group to distinguish facts and sound argument from prejudice and opinions.
10. Call for frequent statements of progress from the discussion recorder.
11. Establish and maintain an informal, cooperative, and permissive group climate.
12. Help the recorder by drawing summary statements from the group "for the record."
13. Keep the discussion on the subject and keep it progressing toward the objective established by the group.
14. Make suggestions instead of giving directions.
15. Stimulate and maintain a spontaneous exchange of ideas and of thinking.

When necessary bring in humor to enliven the atmosphere — but this kind isn't recommended.

16. When necessary bring in appropriate humor to enliven the atmosphere.
17. Translate poorly worded statements into clear statements that communicate.

Good Members Will:

1. Prepare for the discussion in advance of the meeting if possible.
2. Contribute to the discussion and assume any role the group needs to have filled.
3. Help the group define its discussion goal or purpose.
4. Encourage participation and help keep the atmosphere permissive.
5. Supply or seek facts and opinions when needed by the group.
6. Put personally centered roles aside and admit error if the situation demands.
7. Try to understand what other members say and also what they mean.
8. Encourage the group and consciously try to build a feeling of "we-ness."
9. Assume leadership responsibility when necessary.
10. Accept the conclusions of the group if arrived at by democratic processes.
11. Confine remarks to short periods of time. Two to three minutes is the maximum time for a contribution.
12. Express views and ideas without waiting to be prodded by the leader or other members.

A Good Recorder Will:

1. Meet with the leader and other members of the discussion leadership team in advance and discuss the function of the team and particularly the recorder in the group.

2. Record the sense of the discussion, not every word that is spoken.

3. Note the issues and questions discussed, the decisions reached, the proportion of the group in agreement, and significant minority opinions. Ask for clarification of ideas, decisions, etc., for the record.

4. Ask the leader to poll the group if in doubt whether an idea or statement should be recorded. Make sure agreements, disagreements, or decisions actually exist or are made.

5. Remind the group when they get off the subject. This assists the leader in keeping discussion "on the beam."

6. Report on discussion progress during a discussion period when called upon by the leader or group members. Make a summary of main points, agreements, disagreements, and decisions at the close of the meeting.

7. Work with the discussion leader, the observer, and the resource personnel as a member of a team.

8. Edit and prepare a copy of the discussion notes for the record as soon as possible.

The Observer Will:

1. Serve on the leadership team with the special assignment of viewing the group in action and reporting his findings.

2. Meet with the other members of the discussion leadership team and discuss the function and operation of each member of the team.

3. Observe what is happening during the discussion and report this to the group.

4. Examine objectively the group's method of procedure and operation — how the group works rather than what it does.

5. Help the group function more effectively by supplying insights into the operations of the group process.

6. Keep removed from participation in the discussion.

7. Describe for the group the process being used as it works.

8. Make an oral report to the group, describing and summarizing how the group is operating (how the dynamics of the group are being utilized). The decision on how and when this should be done should be reached with the leader.

9. Stimulate the group to evaluate its patterns of operation and to work toward more efficient operation.

The Consultant Will:

1. Contribute relevant facts, points of view, and experiences to the group when and as they are needed.

2. State facts and views as contributions to the discussion, rather than as final thought on the ideas under discussion.

3. As a general rule contribute when requested to do so by the leader or other members of the group.

4. Volunteer when confident the contribution will help move the group toward its objective.

5. Help the group at the close of a discussion to supplement the results and record of their discussion.

6. Be prepared at the close of a discussion to suggest further steps for the group to take in their discussions or in applying their conclusions in follow-up action.

7. Work closely with the discussion leader, observe, and record as a member of the leadership team.

Work closely with the discussion leader, observer, and recorder as a member of the team.

CAUTIONS

1. There must be a problem to be solved or interrelationships to be found.
2. The results or accomplishments of discussion are related directly to the preparation of the group members with facts, general information, and ideas about the problem being discussed.
3. A discussion group is no place to keep ideas a secret; each member must be willing to share information.
4. Good discussion is based on and requires objective thinking.
5. Discussion that follows the steps of problem solving and decision making is more effective than unorganized and random discussion.
6. Listening is vital to discussion; each member must

hear every other member and do some thinking about what he hears.

7. Good discussion depends upon individual contributions.

8. The designated leader must be qualified and have the necessary experience and training to lead a group discussion successfully.

9. The domination of discussion by one or more persons will limit the effectiveness and use of this technique.

2.

The "Huddle" Method
(Discussion 66 or Phillips 66)

THIS DEVICE for breaking down a large group into small units to facilitate discussion was described and popularized by J. Donald Phillips, of Michigan State University. The alternative names are derived from the idea of six persons discussing a subject for six minutes. Essentially it consists of a division of any group into small groups of four to six members for discussion purposes.

DYNAMIC CHARACTERISTICS OF THIS METHOD

1. It allows for the creation of an informal atmosphere no matter how large the group.
2. It permits participation of all those present.
3. It stimulates pooling of ideas within the small group and by means of the reporting to the large group facilitates over-all communication and participation.
4. It encourages a division of labor and responsibility.

5. It secures maximum total individual identification with the subject-problem at hand.
6. It is a rapid method of obtaining consensus.
7. It encourages the development of individual confidence in the democratic process.
8. It makes it very difficult for discussion and recommendations to be controlled by authoritarian leaders or by small vociferous minorities.
9. It helps to free individuals of their inhibitions against participation by identifying their ideas with a small group which then may become the protagonist.
10. The method often provides welcome relief from fatigue, boredom and monotony as large meetings seem to bog down.

THIS METHOD MIGHT BE CHOSEN . . .

1. To obtain information *from* the group, as to their interests, needs, problems, desires, and suggestions to be used in the planning of programs, activities, evaluation procedures, and policies.
2. To arouse audience interest at the outset of a program. Group interest, concern, and identification can be rapidly built up by this method and a mental set for listening and learning may be established. The results of such discussions may or may not be communicated to the speakers.
3. To increase involvement subsequent to various types of presentation. This may take the form of requests for clarification or further information, for attempts to apply general principles to specific situations or to other ways of internalizing the subject matter. It often leads to useful suggestions for action or final solutions.

THIS METHOD IS USEFUL . . .

1. When there is a desire to broaden the base of communication and participation.

2. When it is desired to tap the total resources of the group membership in relation to the subject-problem.

3. When there is a need to analyze a complicated problem which can be logically broken into component parts and segments assigned to various huddle groups.

4. When it seems desirable to broaden responsibility by securing participation of every member. This can be expanded in scope by the assignment of separate segments to various groups and the assignment of specific roles to various individuals within each group.

5. When it seems important to create an informal, permissive, democratic atmosphere.

6. When the rapid pooling of ideas from a large group is needed.

7. When there is a desire to obtain consensus, or to determine if consensus exists.

8. When it is desirable to create individual identity with the group or its problem.

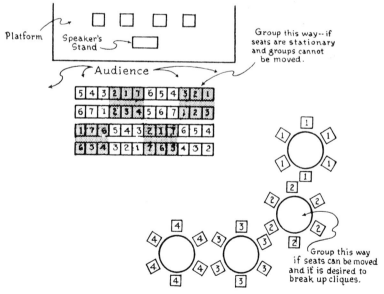

If you plan to use the "huddle," try to utilize your meeting space something like this.

It is difficult to remain anonymous in a group of six.

9. When it seems worthwhile to try to develop individual security and confidence in problem solving and the democratic process. Such confidence gained in the huddle situation may extend to his participation in the total group situation. It is difficult to remain anonymous in a group of six.

10. When it is desired that the democratic process be bolstered in relation to possible authoritarian control.

11. When it seems advisable to stimulate motivation by a change of techniques.

12. When it appears that individual needs and interests are not being well expressed or met in the larger group situation.

13. When group standards and social controls are inadequate in the larger group and it is difficult to maintain thought and discussion at a suitable level. The huddle is a "forcing" situation for thought and discussion.

14. When one wishes to take full advantage of the heterogeneity of the group. Those with varying levels of experience, knowledge or background are much more willing to speak up in the small group; to express minority ideas.

15. When communication and human relations skills are obviously not well distributed within the larger group.

16. When subject matter is of such nature as to make it more easily discussed in a small group.

HOW TO USE THIS METHOD
The Group Should:

1. Have clearly in mind the objectives of the meeting and the segment of the meeting in which the technique will be appropriate.
2. Consider any alternate means which might produce equally good results.
3. Thoroughly think through the purposes for which the method is to be used.
4. Have the questions to be asked of the huddle groups prepared in advance; written on cards if need be.

The Group Leader Should . . .

1. Explain the procedure to the entire group — why it is being used, the mechanics involved, the time to be allowed, the expectations from the method.
2. Make the division into the huddle groups. Often this can be done by prior seating arrangements, but at times a "counting off" or other method may be necessary. This is an efficient way to break up cliques.
3. Give such general instructions as: Get acquainted with each other. Select a chairman to encourage interaction within the huddle. Select a recorder-spokesman to keep a record and to report back to the general meeting. Allow about two minutes for carrying out these procedures.
4. Ask the chairman and the spokesman to identify themselves to make sure this instruction has been carried out.
5. Preferably hand out written copies of the questions to be discussed.
6, Repeat the time allowance and suggest that some comment be obtained from each member. Ask for and answer any questions which have arisen.
7. Move among the groups so as to be available for clari-

fication and to determine progress being made. If it seems desirable the time may be extended, but a one minute warning should be given before calling time.

8. If the number of huddles, or lack of time, precludes a complete report back, ask the groups to take two minutes to rank their ideas in order of importance and pertinence.

9. Collect the reports from each group (written or verbal), classify them and prepare a summary. The procedure at this point develops infinite variety as a result of size of meeting, types of questions discussed, use to be made of them, etc.

10. Make an attempt to 'see that all significant points of view are brought before the general body in one form or another.

CAUTIONS

1. This method has little value in disseminating information except as it taps the knowledge and experience of the individual group members.

2. The method tends to be overused by those who have experienced success with it. Like any other technique, it is useful only for certain purposes and under certain conditions.

3. The mechanical problems involved are formidable; rigorous prior planning is called for to minimize them.

4. Huddle groups cannot produce above the level of knowledge and experience possessed by the individuals. It is well to be realistic regarding results expected.

5. Time limitation and reporting back are essential features of the technique, but too much emphasis on them may hamper discussion.

6. Failure to make adequate use of the material obtained may create frustration among those who worked hard to produce it.

3.

The "Buzz Group" Method

AN ALTERNATIVE METHOD of breaking a large group into small segments to facilitate discussion is called the "buzz group" technique. Although the term is sometimes used interchangeably with "huddles" or "discussion 66" it is reserved in this instance for *two-person* discussion groups. Since many of the characteristics and basic elements of this method are identical with those of the "huddle," only the exceptions and the relatively unique aspects will be noted.

DYNAMIC CHARACTERISTICS OF THIS METHOD

1. It is an extremely informal device.
2. It virtually guarantees total participation.
3. It has even greater potential for total individual involvement than the huddle method.

4. It is usually practicable for groups of fifty or less.
5. It is extremely easy to set up.

THIS METHOD MIGHT BE CHOSEN . . .

1. To provide maximum opportunity for individual participation in an informal setting.
2. To consider many separate aspects of a subject-problem.
3. To provide limited support to individuals for the purpose of facilitating their participation in the total group process.
4. To give opportunity for the widest possible expression of the heterogeneous characteristics of the members with respect to background, knowledge, or point of view.

HOW TO USE THIS METHOD

1. A simple "count off" procedure is usually all that is needed to set up the groups. No movement of people is ordinarily involved.
2. There need be no chairman, but agree on who is to report the results of the discussion.
3. Instructions and procedure can be greatly simplified as compared to the huddle technique.

CAUTIONS

1. Because a large number of persons may be talking at once a high noise level may develop. It may prove necessary to warn against this or even to alter the physical setting.
2. Group standards and the levels of social controls are usually not as high in this informal setting.
3. There is always the possibility that one of the two members of the buzz group will dominate the other

and completely submerge any contribution which he might make.

4. There may be wide variations in the time required to cover a subject between the various buzz groups. The time allowance can usually be somewhat shorter than when six persons must air their views.

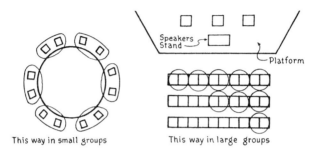

This way in small groups   This way in large groups

The "buzz group" method may be used by both large and small groups.

4.

The Symposium

A GROUP OF TALKS, speeches, or lectures presented by several individuals on the various phases of a single subject-problem is called a symposium. A moderator often controls time and subject matter. Properly used, the talks should be limited to not more than twenty minutes and the total time of the symposium should not exceed one hour.

DYNAMIC CHARACTERISTICS OF THIS METHOD

1. This is a relatively formal method of presentation and is comparatively easy to organize.
2. It allows for a systematic and relatively complete expression of ideas in an uninterrupted fashion.
3. By it, complex subjects and problems may be divided readily into logical component parts.

4. Structuring of the presentation may be obtained readily by agreement among the participants prior to the symposium.
5. There should be a minimum of duplication and repetition and time allotments should lead to precise, logical presentations.
6. Excellent control of the subject matter, as well as of the length of the symposium, may be attained by mutual agreements among the participants made prior to the symposium.
7. It must depend upon empathy with the speaker or subject matter, or upon competitive points of view, to develop audience interest and involvement. Hence, it has limited usefulness in this respect.
8. There is a minimum of interaction between the participants.

THIS METHOD MIGHT BE CHOSEN . . .

1. To present basic information — facts or points of view.

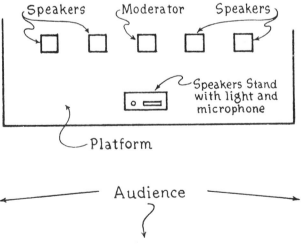

A suggested platform arrangement for the symposium.

2. To present a relatively complete and systematic expression of ideas without interruption.
3. To break down a relatively complex subject-problem on the basis of:
   a. its logical component parts
   b. different points of view or special interests
   c. alternative proposed solutions and their consequences.
4. When there needs to be a relatively high degree of control over logical breakdown of the subject-problem, the subject matter discussed and the timing.
5. To bring together and focus different points of view within a logical, more generalized framework or context.

THIS METHOD IS USEFUL . . .

1. When group objectives, or objective of the specific meeting or meeting segment, can be accurately communicated to the speakers.
2. When the group standards, social control, and identity are such that the more formal means of presentation — the symposium technique — is acceptable to the group.
3. When formality in presentation is not a major hindrance to group listening and learning.
4. When one is relatively sure that the level of communication used by the speakers will be understandable to the group.
5. When group members have the ability and skills to take related ideas presented in different speech segments, by different people, and integrate them into a meaningful whole.
6. When the presentation of different points of view represented in a heterogeneous group is thought to be necessary.
7. When interaction among participants is not thought to be necessary.

8. When it is believed that the group is not mature enough to handle differences in opinions and/or conflict situations which may arise in open discussion of the subject-problem among group members.
9. When the size of the group is too large to allow for total group involvement and there is a desire to present different points of view.

HOW TO USE THIS METHOD
The Group Should:
1. Have clearly in mind the objectives of the meeting and the particular segment of the meeting in which this technique might be used.
2. Consider alternative means that might be used to accomplish this objective.
3. Decide in general terms how the subject-problem should be analyzed.

The Moderator or Chairman Should:
1. Meet with the symposium speakers well before the meeting and secure agreement on the logical breakdown of the subject-problem, outline the general areas to be covered by each symposium member, agree on sequence of appearance, and decide on time allowances.
2. Meet with the symposium speakers immediately before the meeting to review above points.
3. At the meeting give the general setting of the subject-problem to be discussed and point out its significance. Describe the logical breakdown of the problem into the component parts to be discussed by each symposium speaker. Set an atmosphere for attentive listening and thinking by the total group.
4. Briefly introduce symposium speakers.
5. Inform the group of the procedure to be followed, including the role of the symposium speakers and the role of the group during and after the formal symposium.

6. Introduce each speaker more in detail as his turn comes on the symposium and establish the qualification of the speakers to speak on the subject assigned. Make needed transitional statements to "carry" the audience logically from one speaker to the next.
7. Perform additional functions depending on what procedure has been set up to follow the formal symposium, including summarization or any of these alternative follow-up techniques:
    a. Give each speaker time for a short statement of clarification and/or rebuttal.
    b. Allow each speaker to ask one or two questions of any of the other speakers.
    c. Convert the formal symposium group into a panel for additional discussion.
    d. Involve the audience in direct questioning from the floor or in a forum discussion.

Symposium Speakers Should:

1. Attend the planning meetings indicated above.
2. Prepare concise, well-organized presentations that can be given within the time allotted.
3. Present prepared material clearly and concisely in the allotted time.

CAUTIONS

1. Use special care in choosing the subject-problem and breaking the topic down into its meaningful and manageable component parts.
2. Careful selection is important in naming the moderator and the symposium speakers. Unbiased members who can approach their assignment logically and make their presentation without over-emotional involvement are important. The moderator is just that — not a speech maker, rebuttalist, or interpreter of symposium speeches.

3. In preplanning, limit the time of the speeches and set a method for enforcing the time limitation. Symposiums tend to run on and on.
4. While logical, precise presentations are the key to good symposiums, the interest of the larger group must be stimulated and maintained if the symposium is to fulfill its objective.

5.

The Panel Discussion

A DISCUSSION before an audience by a selected group of persons (usually three to six) under a moderator is called a panel discussion. It might be described as an informal committee discussion overheard by an audience. The form of discussion is conversational — no speeches by members or by the moderator should be permitted.

DYNAMIC CHARACTERISTICS OF THIS METHOD

1. The atmosphere can be informal or formal.
2. Limited control of the scope and direction of discussion can be maintained by prior discussion among the panelists, defining the discussion framework to the audience just before introduction of the panel, or by the activities of the moderator.
3. There can be no complete control by the moderator since the panel members can ignore questions and directions.

4. It can expose and focus on different points of view, different facts, and different attitudes on a subject-problem.

5. It allows for maximum interaction and interstimulation between panel members.

6. It often increases the interest of an audience in the subject because of the active and dramatic presentation of the subject matter, differences of opinion, competition, etc.

7. It is a useful method of defining points of agreement, areas of disagreement, and of approaching consensus.

8. It divides responsibility by requiring some pre-meeting thought and fact gathering from individual panel members.

THIS METHOD MIGHT BE CHOSEN . . .

1. To create an informal atmosphere for communication with the group.

2. To identify the problem or issues to be considered and to explore them.

3. To give the audience an understanding of the component parts of the problem.

4. To get different facts and points of view brought into a discussion framework.

5. To weigh the advantages and disadvantages of a course or courses of action.

There can be no complete control by the moderator since the panel members can ignore questions and directions.

6. To supply facts and opinions about problems and issues.

7. To create audience interest in problems and issues.

8. To motivate the larger group to constructive thought or action.

9. To determine areas of agreement, discuss areas of disagreement and to strive for consensus.

10. To force a group to face a controversial issue and to stimulate them to join in the problem-solving process.

11. To aid a group confronted with a very controversial issue which no one wants to defend or attack — the panel spreads responsibility.

THIS METHOD IS USEFUL . . .

1. When the group is too large for all to be involved.

2. When the group has an interest in the subject and wants to know more about it, but general overt participation is not a primary objective.

3. When the level of group standards is such that the members are willing to listen to both sides of a problem and work for agreement or consensus.

4. When the level of group standards is such that the members are willing to exchange ideas and points of view with other members and to probe deeply into a problem.

5. When the members impanelled are willing and able to communicate with each other and the remainder of the group.

6. When social controls are strong enough that the panel will abide by the rules laid down as to area of discussion, methods of procedure, and the role of the moderator and panel members.

7. When the level of human relations and communication skills of panel members is adequate to facilitate good discussion.

8. When the roles of the moderator, panel members and other group members are within the limits of the general role definitions by the group.
9. When the panel members and/or the moderator have the ability to play unit act roles expected to be needed in the panel discussion.
10. When it is judged there is, or can be created, enough heterogeneity of interests and opinion to make the discussion worthwhile.
11. When heterogeneity in the group makes it advisable to present different points of view or facts in relation to a subject-problem.
12. When conditions exist that make it difficult or impossible for the group as a whole to discuss a controversial issue rationally. There may be members in the group who can bring the discussion to a more rational level when placed on a panel.

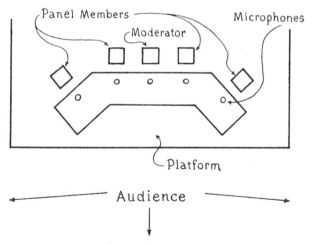

A suggested setup for a panel discussion.

HOW TO USE THIS METHOD
The Group Should:

1. Have clearly in mind the objectives of the meeting and the particular segment of the meeting in which this technique might be used.
2. Consider alternative means that might be used to accomplish this objective.
3. Make sure the group selects a timely and significant topic that lends itself to panel discussion.
4. Select panel members with care. If possible, people should be chosen who are interested in the problem or issue, have facts and/or opinions, represent different views, and have had different experiences. They should be cooperative and willing to express themselves before a group.
5. Select a chairman or moderator who has the respect of the panel, who will not take sides, who can think rapidly and clearly, ask pertinent, reflective questions, and can summarize well.
6. Select panel members and the moderator far enough in advance to give them an opportunity for study and thought before the presentation.
7. Seat panel members around a table in such a way that they can look at and talk with one another and yet easily see and be seen by the audience.

The Chairman Should:

1. Plan the meeting and make all necessary arrangements.
2. Open the meeting and welcome the group.
3. Introduce the moderator.
4. Close the meeting.
5. The chairman may double as moderator.

The Moderator Should:

1. Meet with the panel members before the meeting and coordinate the prospective program — agree upon the scope of the discussion; divide the general problem into discussible areas; assign rough time limits for each phase of the proposed discussion; assign special, individual responsibilities where necessary; and prepare some form of group outline or discussion plan. Often two meetings will be required.
2. Make sure that the seating arrangement is the best. Do not seat members with similar views together. Seat lively speakers at the ends and quiet ones in the middle so that they may be drawn in.
3. Introduce panel members to the group.
4. Introduce the subject-problem to the general group, secure the interest of the group, and prepare the way for the discussion to follow. Explain the procedure to be followed in the meeting, indicating whether and in what way the full group will have an opportunity to participate.
5. Open the discussion with a question or statement that will immediately focus attention on the central point of interest.

Seat lively speakers at the ends and quiet ones in the middle . . . .

6. Draw the entire panel into informal, conversational discussion.
7. Enter the discussion to (1) ask clarifying questions, (2) interpret uncertain meanings, (3) bring discussion back on the track, (4) summarize, (5) close off areas of discussion and move ahead, (6) ask "next step" questions, and (7) interrupt speechmakers. The moderator does not express his opinion.
8. Ask reflective thought questions — not yes or no questions.
9. Work toward basic understanding but also probe for points of disagreement for additional discussion.
10. Let participation be as free and spontaneous as possible. Address questions to the panel as a whole or to a part of it, not to individual members, except for clarification of statements already made or to bring special facts or points of view into the discussion.
11. Present a final summary.
12. Turn the meeting back to the chairman if a chairman is used, or close the meeting himself.

The Panel Member Should:

1. Prepare material and organize thoughts on the discussion topic.
2. Set an example of careful, reflective, and rational thinking.
3. Listen thoughtfully to the comments of the other panel members and strive to get their viewpoints and what lies back of them.
4. Express views and ideas vigorously, clearly, concisely.
5. Watch for the right moment to present his viewpoint.
6. Change his views if logic or data prove his position in error.
7. Speak only on the topic under consideration.

8. Confine remarks to short periods of time. Two or three minutes is considered to be the *maximum* time for each contribution.
9. Keep the atmosphere of the discussion informal and conversational.
10. Contribute to the clarity and unity of the discussion by restating others' views more clearly, reducing overstatements, pointing out unanimity when it exists, recognizing the presence or absence of substantiation for any point, and shifting the direction of discussion in case of an impasse.
11. Help the leader draw in other members of the panel.

CAUTIONS

1. The success of this technique depends in a large measure on the moderator and the panel members — they must be carefully selected.
2. The discussion must not be monopolized by one or two members.
3. Pre-meeting planning is an absolute necessity for success but—
4. There should be no preliminary "dry-run" discussion of the subject. If this is done the public discussion often becomes an anticlimax — stale and stagey. Prepare a simple, short outline of the points to cover.
5. Allow enough time — panels shorter than 30 minutes seldom succeed — but conclude while general group interest is still high.

TECHNIQUE

6.

The Interrogator Panel

THIS METHOD is an interrogation-discussion interchange between a small group of knowledgeable individuals (the panel) and one or more other persons (the interrogators), often under the direction of a moderator. This variation on the usual panel technique is a most effective method of making use of experts and resource personnel. Ordinarily the panel consists of three to five members and a single interrogator is used to propound questions to them. The interchange is at the conversational level, but the answers are expected to be as precise as possible. It is a highly effective method for obtaining specific information on a specific topic. It is obviously more of an informational or educational technique than one designed to lead directly to action.

DYNAMIC CHARACTERISTICS OF THIS METHOD

1. Many questions can be covered in a short period.
2. The interaction between the interrogator and the panel should lead to the full development of a subject.
3. Limited control of the direction and scope of the discussion may be maintained. Preliminary agreement as to the general areas to be covered may involve the interrogator, the panel, a committee, or an entire group. Further control can be obtained by the use of a moderator.
4. Control can never be complete, since all participants must have freedom to act.
5. A high interest level is usually obtained as a result of the implied competitive atmosphere created.
6. Specificity of questions and answers is probably higher under this technique than any other.

THIS METHOD MIGHT BE CHOSEN . . .

1. To make use of the superior knowledge or experience of certain individuals.
2. To explore many facets of a complex problem.
3. To stimulate interest in the details of a current problem.
4. To obtain detailed facts from the experts.

THIS METHOD IS USEFUL . . .

1. When the group is too large to permit general questioning of a panel.
2. When a group is interested enough to explore a subject in greater depth than their own resources permit.
3. When the group is amenable to hearing a variety of viewpoints.
4. When consultants can be obtained who will receive general acceptance by the group.

5. When competent interrogators, moderators, or panel members are available within the group and are acceptable to the group.

HOW TO USE THIS METHOD
The Group Should:

1. Determine what objectives may be accomplished by the method and at what point it should be used.
2. In terms of the other known techniques, decide if this one has the most potential for achieving the intended goal or goals.
3. Delineate the general area in which answers will be sought.
4. Choose the interrogator(s) with care. They should be able to ask questions in such a way that panel members will have no doubt that they are straight information-seeking remarks with no intent to build logical traps or clinch debators' points. The interrogators must have the ability to adequately and accurately phrase questions which will bring forth the information that they are seeking.
5. Choose panel members who can think rapidly and say precisely what they think. The good resource people are not readily flustered by rapid interchanges of ideas. Panel members on the same resource unit should not vary widely in ability to communicate or in level of knowledge. In such situations the superior individual will either "under perform" in deference to

Choose panel members who . . . can command the language to say precisely what they think.

his counterpart or go at his regular pace and cause embarrassment by invidious comparisons being made. The inferior individual, in protecting his ego, may engage in diverting tactics which makes the attainment of the interrogators' goals difficult. Thus impact can be lost.

6. Choose a moderator who understands the technique and who is willing to accept the role.

7. Select all panel personnel far enough in advance of the meeting to give them a chance to determine what answers are needed to help the group toward its goals and to get these answers.

8. Create an adequate physical setting. Panel should sit so that they can see the audience, the interrogator, and the moderator. A commonly used arrangement is to place tables so that they form a wedge pointing toward the rear of the platform. The moderator sits

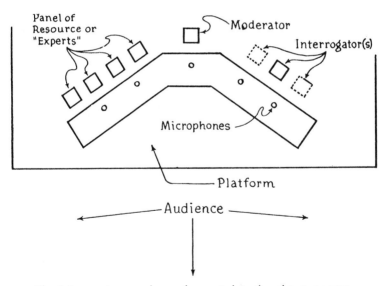

The interrogator panel may be seated in the above manner.

at the point of the wedge and has the interrogator(s) on one wing and the panel members on the other. (Figure 7).

9. Select a chairman to plan the meeting (with committee if needed) and make all the necessary mechanical arrangements such as seeing that tables are ordered, lighting is adequate, etc. He will also call meeting to order, introduce the general topic and the moderator, and close the meeting.

The Moderator Should:

1. Meet with the interrogators(s) and the chairman, and in some cases panel members, to determine how the line of questioning will be established. One alternative is to accept the definition of the problem by the chairman, moderator, and the interrogator(s). Another alternative is to use some group technique such as buzz, huddle, or more commonly, a request for individual submission of questions. The latter may be done at the same meeting or it may be done at a preceding meeting. If it is done at the same meeting the panel has little time to organize the questions, but the group is already involved and the members are mentally set to hear answers.

2. Introduce the interrogator(s) and panel members to the group as a whole.

3. Introduce the subject matter in enough detail to establish the position into which the interrogator panel fits in relation to the total goal orientation of the group. A good introduction is like a bathing suit — it covers the essentials but is brief enough to cause interest.

4. Explain the procedure to be followed so that the panel and the group as a whole do not get lost in the mechanics of the technique.

5. Open the discussion by posing a general question which starts the discussion and the subsequent questioning of the panel.

6. Decide who shall have precedence if two interrogators are attempting to ask questions at once, taking into consideration the pertinence of the questions and the relative dominance of the questioners.

7. Intervene when needed to: (a) seek further clarification of a point under discussion, (b) press for further interpretation if he thinks it is necessary, (c) rule out a question because of its irrelevance to the issue, (d) stop the response of the panel members if the response is obviously irrelevant, (e) ask for repetition of a question or answer if the interrogator and panel members appear to be "talking by" each other, (f) close off areas of discussion to move ahead, (g) interrupt the interrogator if he makes speeches or otherwise misinterprets his role, (h) interrupt a panel member if the answer appears redundant or too lengthy for the question which sought it.

8. Close off the questioning, present a final summary, and thank the participants for their cooperation.

9. Turn the meeting back to chairman.

A Good Interrogator Should:

1. Organize questions which will bring out the points and clarifications desired from the panel.

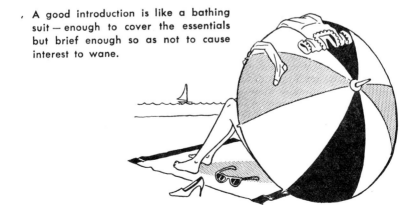

, A good introduction is like a bathing suit — enough to cover the essentials but brief enough so as not to cause interest to wane.

2. Conduct himself in such a manner that the panel members will feel free to give frank and straightforward answers to questions.

3. Exercise the usual good manners of conventional discussion.

4. Listen carefully to answers of panel members in order to avoid duplication and waste of time.

5. Express questions in clear, concise and friendly manner without the use of techniques which will distract the group as a whole or the panel members.

6. Represent the interests of the group in seeking answers to as many questions as possible.

7. Remember that in this technique he has the primary responsibility while the technique is in process for the direction and effectiveness of the outcome, i.e. the learning experiences of the group. The moderator can give guidance only by interrupting and redirecting. The panel members have the responsibility only to answer the questions posed them.

8. Observe the panel process and make certain that the key questions which were discussed in the group prior to its access to the panel get asked.

The Panel Members (Experts) Should:

1. Learn the area of questioning which will be covered and also whether the group wants facts, opinions, or both.

2. Clearly indicate to the group when they are dealing with facts and when with opinions.

3. Be prepared to do the job expected or decline the invitation to appear on the program.

4. Give answers in precise, clear terms and as briefly as possible.

5. Carefully stick to giving answers to the questions asked and not use the situation as an opportunity to expound a personal "pet project."

CAUTIONS

1. For maximum value, use the technique in conjunction with other techniques which involve the total group in devising questions or lines of questioning to be used.
2. The technique, while it provides for details on a problem and gets answers to specific questions of the group, is quite time consuming.
3. Use panel members (resource people) who have a high level of human relations skills and an ability to shift their patterns of thought rapidly in line with the nature of the questioning.
4. The successful use of this method depends heavily upon the ability of the interrogator(s). The moderator has limited control of direction, but the interrogator, by his questions, gives major direction to the discussion.
5. Premeeting planning is a necessity for success. It is desirable for the moderator to meet with both the interrogator and the panel. With the interrogator he makes certain that there is an understanding of the area in which questions will be asked and the kinds of specific questions to which the group wants answers. With the panel members he explains the areas in which questions will be asked and how much time is available. He urges them to be brief and definite.
6. A "dry-run" of the discussion is never desirable.
7. The interchange will be stimulated if the interrogator is given a few minutes to visit with the panel prior to the meeting, and if the moderator goes over the ground rules informally with them before going on the platform.

TECHNIQUE

7.

The Committee Hearing

THE QUESTIONING of an individual by several persons constitutes the group technique known as the committee hearing. In its formal style, as practiced by various committees of Congress, it has been made familiar to nearly everyone through the medium of television. It can be used much less formally as a group method by setting up a committee of members to obtain information from a consultant for the benefit of the entire group. Such a committee forms a bridge between the group and the expert.

DYNAMIC CHARACTERISTICS OF THIS METHOD

1. It is essentially a formal method.
2. It permits rather flexible control of the situation by the committee.
3. Interest is usually high because of the verbal interplay

between questioners and expert. This can be further increased to the point of deep psychological involvement by means of establishing a competitive atmosphere.

4. As compared to the interview, which it resembles, the committee hearing makes much greater use of variations in knowledge, skills, and abilities of the questioners.

5. Good questioning is often obtained because of the mutual support and sharing of responsibility afforded the committee members.

6. It encourages cooperative thinking and questioning.

7. Each questioner has time to consider his questions while another has the floor.

An atmosphere of "closeness" . . . can be created between the group and the speaker.

THIS METHOD MIGHT BE CHOSEN . . .

1. To stimulate interest or obtain information, facts, opinions, or policy pronouncements in a total group setting and in context meaningful to the group. Especially when there is a desire to probe deeply in certain areas, this technique can be used for many purposes varying from informal gathering of experience information to questioning "hostile witnesses" regarding administrative policy or stands on political issues.

2. To create a psychological bridge between the speaker or resource person and the group — the questioning committee from the group can often perform this function. An atmosphere of "closeness" or group representation can be created between the group and the questioners.

3. To help make better use of a speaker or consultant who:
   a. Has difficulty expressing himself before a group in a lecture setting.
   b. Tends to be verbose and rambling — has difficulty organizing his presentation.
   c. Has difficulty speaking to the level of the group.
   d. Tends to be evasive, develops his points too rapidly for the group, or is superficial on certain critical points of information or opinion.
   e. Has difficulty judging the interest and concern areas of the group.
   f. Is so clever with words or argumentative techniques that he would be difficult for any one member of the group to handle in an interview situation.

4. To question in a logical organized fashion. A questioning committee will probably come closer to meeting this criterion than the entire group would.

5. To conserve time in the meeting.

6. To conserve time for preparation — the questioning

committee can meet together and then meet with the consultant to organize the presentation.

THIS METHOD IS USEFUL . . .

1. When the objectives of the group or of the particular meeting are difficult to explain to an outside speaker or resource person.
2. When the more conventional methods of the speaker, a lecturer, or general discussion do not appear to be the best means.
3. When there is need for the role of a psychological bridge between the speaker or resource person and the group.
4. When group standards and social control in the group are not at a level so the group as a whole will obtain the desired information from the speaker or resource person.

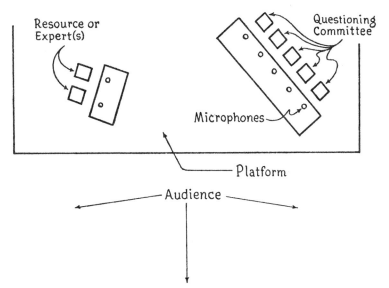

Seating for a committee hearing may be arranged in this manner.

5. When an individual member of the group or the group as a whole does not have the human relations and communications skills to obtain the desired information from a speaker or resource person, it is possible that a small group of members (the questioning committee) would possess the needed skills.

6. When it is desirable to establish a permissive atmosphere and communication pattern with the speaker or resource person that will lead to greater participation by group members in subsequent questioning and discussion.

7. When the size of the group is too large for effective group questioning of the speaker or resource person, but where there is a desire to involve directly several people in a direct participation role (questioning committee).

8. When it is believed that each individual, or the questioning committee as a group, have greater skills than does the group as a whole at playing unit act roles that will lead to more effective use of the speaker or resource person.

9. When there is some degree of heterogeneity of interests or points of view in the group and there is a desire to represent several of them in the questioning.

10. When group standards are such that all group members will not assume the responsibility for thinking through a line of questioning to be used with the speaker or resource person. This responsibility can be given to the questioning committee.

11. When the individual group members feel insecure in the position of the role of questioning an expert. There may be certain group members that will feel secure in this role and can be used as the questioning committee. In some cases individual members may feel insecure and not perform the questioning function if the group as a whole is to ask questions, but

if given the assignment by the group will attempt to perform the questioning function.

12. When it may be desirable to avoid feelings of aggression and projection against the expert. To keep these at a minimum it may be decided to choose a questioning committee that will probably be rational in their questioning.

HOW TO USE THIS METHOD
The Group Should:

1. Have clearly in mind the objective(s) of the meeting and the particular segment of the meeting in which this technique might be used.

2. Consider alternative means that might be used to accomplish this objective.

3. Secure a qualified subject-problem expert. Such a person will usually come from outside the group but may be a member of the group.

4. Secure a questioning committee — capable as secure individuals in human relations and communication skills and subject matter. Usually they will be members of the group. However, in some cases it may be well to have one or more of the questioning committee be people from outside the group if they have specific questioning abilities or subject or authority competence needed by the group.

5. The questioning committee should meet and think through the important aspects of the problem, the framework for questioning, the important areas for questioning, the level of questioning, the procedure, and timing. The questioning committee may wish to involve the entire group in suggesting significant areas for questioning.

6. The expert and the questioning committee should usually meet in advance of the meeting and decide the general framework for questioning, the major

areas of questioning, the procedure to be followed, and timing. This should enable the expert to refresh his memory, secure additional information, and organize his thinking. It may open up new avenues of questioning for the questioning committee.

7. Definite assignments should be made on who is to: introduce the expert and the committee, give the background on the area to be discussed, set the framework and procedure for listening, and define the role of the remainder of the group during and following the hearing.

8. In some cases, the expert may be allowed to make a brief formal statement at the beginning of the hearing.

9. The qualifications of the expert should be established in the introduction or early in the committee hearing.

10. The questioning committee should always keep in mind, and in fact may want to assign specific tasks to committee members, the unit act roles that need to be performed if the hearing is going to be most meaningful to the group — orienter, clarifier, integrator, energizer, harmonizer, summarizer, etc.

11. There may be need to assign someone the specific role of final summarizer. It may be a member of the questioning committee, the chairman, or a group member given the specific assignment of determining significant facts, opinions, agreements, or differences of opinions and reporting them to the group for discussion or acceptance.

12. The questioning committee should strive to establish themselves with the entire group as their representatives in the committee hearing situation.

13. Attention should be given to the physical setting of the meeting. The arrangement should be such that everyone can see and hear. Different psychological effects can be obtained by the relative placing of the

expert, the questioning committee, and the remainder of the group. For instance, it is possible to create the impression of committee dominance by placing the committee on a raised platform which allows its members to look down to the person being questioned. Place the remainder of the group in a semicircle so that they can see both the expert and the questioning committee. For a more permissive atmosphere place the expert among the questioning committee members with the remainder of the group distributed in an informal arrangement around them.

CAUTIONS

1. Select the expert with care. A reluctant or insecure expert may contribute little to the meeting.
2. The questioning committee should carefully plan their questioning. Unorganized questioning will probably not produce much significant information. This does not mean that the committee should not be flexible in following up significant leads.
3. Beware of the dominant position that the questioning committee may have over the individual expert. Depending on the objective of using the committee hearing technique the degree to which this potential dominance is used should be kept in mind.
4. The questioning committee should always remember that they are representing the group as a whole. Thus questioning should be in line with the groups' interests and concerns and at a level and at the speed of idea development understandable to the group.

The Dialogue

A DISCUSSION carried on in front of a group by two knowledgeable people capable of thoughtful communicative discourse on a specific subject is called a dialogue. It is less formal than a lecture or a panel discussion and has many unique dynamics of its own.

DYNAMIC CHARACTERISTICS OF THIS METHOD

1. It can be very informal and conversational.
2. It allows direct and easy communication of information and points of view by the dialogue members, usually experts.
3. It allows for mutual support and sharing of responsibility between two people.
4. It allows for interpersonal stimulation.
5. It aids unskilled speakers in presenting their ideas.

6. It usually creates great interest among other members of the group.
7. It is simple in form and easy to plan and carry out.
8. It allows for clarification, logic, validation, and consistency as the discussion develops; and permits expression of two points of view.
9. It allows for control of the framework of the discussion but also permits flexibility as the discussion progresses — cues from group reaction may be "picked up" by the participants.
10. Responsibility can be given to at least two group members for thought and fact gathering before a meeting.

THIS METHOD MIGHT BE CHOSEN . . .

1. To present facts, opinions, or points of view in an informal, conversational manner.
2. To create interest in a subject.
3. To focus attention on an issue or problem.
4. To explore in detail different points of view or obtain agreement on two or more points of view.

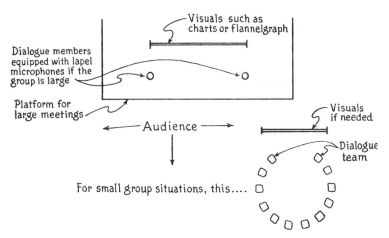

The dialogue method may be used before both large and small groups.

5. To create a desire and motivation for reflective thinking.
6. To rapidly set a framework for thought and discussion and give basic facts preparatory to general group discussion — a dialogue can often remove a controversial issue from the emotional group discussion setting and thus enable the group to approach the subject-problem on a more rational basis.

THIS METHOD IS USEFUL . . .

1. When group standards, identity, and social controls are such that there will be group attention to the dialogue and identity with the participants.
2. When knowledgeable people have the skills to play unit act roles to a sufficient degree to produce a good discussion. In some situations certain people have status and capabilities that lead the group to better thinking and group productivity.
3. When the appearance of group members or outsiders in the role of dialogue discussants is acceptable to the group.
4. When knowledgeable people are available who are roughly comparable in knowledge of the subject-problem, in their ability to communicate in a reflective, stimulating manner, and who are able to work together as a team.
5. When groups have a low level of participation it is often chosen to stimulate thought, create a discussion atmosphere, and lead to participation.
6. When there is a group atmosphere favorable to acceptance of ideas or stimulation from persons isolated from a total group discussion.
7. When working with a smaller group than might be a desirable size for a symposium or panel, but also useful for very large groups.

8. When knowledgeable people do not have the degree of security or necessary skills to give a lecture or lead a discussion.
9. When the group identifies well with the problem and/or members of the dialogue team.
10. When it seems desirable to motivate able members in order to facilitate a higher level of interest, thought, and participation on their part — there is usually a high degree of interstimulation between the dialogue team members.

HOW TO USE THIS METHOD
The Group Should:

1. Select a timely and significant topic with which at least two group members (or outside resource people) are familiar.
2. Select dialogue team members. They should be able to work as a team, share leadership, guide the conversation, integrate, summarize, and provide transitions and timing.
3. Decide on the person — perhaps the chairman of the meeting — to introduce the dialogue, to take responsibility for receiving questions after the dialogue, and to lead the discussion.

The Participants Should:

1. Arrange a meeting (or meetings, if needed) before the presentation at which an agreement should be reached on:
   a. The framework for discussion and the general area to be covered with a tentative outline;
   b. How the subject will be introduced and how the framework for discussion set;
   c. Tentative timing by major points;
   d. Responsibilities for summarizing and integrating and transitions from point to point.

2. Arrange the physical setting so that all group members can see, hear, and feel a part of the dialogue situation — try to create an air of "eavesdropping."
3. Fulfill the designated roles objectively and without over-emotional involvement.
4. Return the meeting to the chairman for clarifying questions and summarization.

CAUTIONS

1. The topic should be one in which the group is interested — not only the dialogue participants.
2. Keep the discussion at a level that can be understood by the group — experts may discuss at a level too far above the group.
3. Do not develop the discussion too rapidly. The dialogue participants know more about the subject and have been over it in some detail in their planning meeting — the group members have not.
4. Avoid making "speeches" and reading written material.
5. Share the responsibility; if not, the dialogue may end up as an interview or a series of lengthy speeches.
6. Although the major interaction is between the dialogue participants, they should not get so enamored with each other and their ideas that they forget they must communicate to other group members.

Dialogue participants should not get so enamored with each other that they forget. . . other group members.

9.

The Interview

THE QUESTIONING of an expert on a given subject by an interviewer, who represents the group, is called an interview. The expert is usually, but not necessarily, one from outside the group. The interviewer (questioner) is usually a member of the group. Everyone is familiar with the "interview" as it is heard or seen on radio and television. It has a great potential for use in the formal groups under discussion also.

DYNAMIC CHARACTERISTICS OF THIS METHOD

1. It is less formal than a lecture or a speech, more formal than a dialogue.
2. There is usually mutual support and sharing of responsibility between the expert and interviewer.

3. The interviewer becomes a bridge between the group and the expert.
4. It allows for flexible control by the interviewer, since he sets the level of discussion, the speed with which areas are developed, and the direction of development. It is more difficult for the expert to evade points of interest or concern to the group if the interviewer continues to question in those areas.
5. Verbal interaction usually stimulates the interest of group members. It is possible to set up a competitive situation between the expert and the group figure which can lead to group stimulation and deeper psychological involvement.

THIS METHOD MIGHT BE CHOSEN . . .

1. To stimulate interest or obtain information, facts, opinions, or policy pronouncements, in a context meaningful to the group.
2. To develop one line of thought in a consistent manner. Usually one questioner can better accomplish this goal than general group questioning.
3. To create a psychological bridge between the speaker or resource person and the group — a questioner from the group can often perform this function. An atmosphere of "closeness" can be created between the group and the speaker.
4. To help make better use of a speaker or resource person who feels ill at ease alone before a group, who tends to be evasive on certain critical points of information or opinion, or has difficulty judging the interest and concern areas of the group.
5. To save time in the meeting structuring.
6. To save group time in preparations — an individual from the group can meet with the speaker or resource person to organize the presentation.

THIS METHOD IS USEFUL . . .

1. When the objectives of the group or of the particular meeting are difficult to explain to an outside speaker or resource person.

2. When the more conventional methods do not appear to be the best means — as when group standards and social control in the group are not at such a level that the group will obtain the desired information from a lecture.

3. When there is need for the role of a psychological bridge between the speaker or resource person and the group.

4. When the group members as a whole do not have the human relations or communication skills to get the desired information from the speaker or resource person.

5. When the size of the group is too large for effective group questioning of a resource person or speaker.

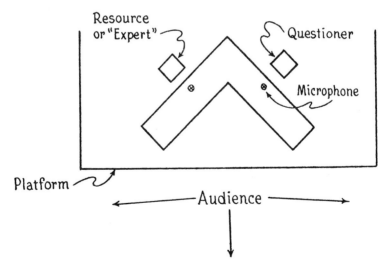

A simple arrangement may be used in staging an interview.

6. When an individual group member is relatively secure and has skills apt to lead to more effective use of a speaker or resource person than do other group members.

HOW TO USE THIS METHOD
The Group Should:

1. Have clearly in mind the objective of the meeting and the particular segment of the meeting in which this technique might be used.
2. Consider alternative means that might be used to accomplish this objective.
3. Secure an expert (usually from outside the group, but such a person may be a member of the group) on the subject-problem of concern.
4. Secure a capable questioner (usually from within the group, but he may be from outside the group).
5. Decide before the meeting time who is going to introduce the expert, the interviewer, and the interview technique and set the scene for the interview and plans for total group involvement following the interview. These functions can be performed by the chairman, the questioner, or some other group member.
6. Attention should be given to the physical setting of the meeting. Make sure all group members can see and hear. Create an air of eavesdropping if possible.

A Good Interviewer Should:

1. Consider the level of questioning, the important aspects of the problem, the framework for discussion, the important areas to be discussed, the procedure, and the timing.
2. Meet with the consultant and decide on the general framework for questioning, the major areas of questioning, the procedure to be followed, and the timing.

3. Keep in mind the unit act roles needed to make the interview meaningful to the group — orienter, clarifier, integrator, summarizer, etc.
4. Strive to establish himself as a representative of the group; to perceive his role as a connector between the expert and the group.

CAUTIONS

1. Keep the interview flexible and conversational.
2. Questions should be reflective — those with a yes or no answer quickly kill interest.
3. Keep questions at the level of the group's ability to understand and develop ideas at a suitable pace.
4. Any speaker may feel that certain questions are inappropriate, or "too hot to handle." Even though the purpose of the interview is to obtain detailed or difficult information, the consultant should be allowed the privilege of refusing to answer.
5. In any interview there must always be a compromise between deep probing on a few points and more superficial coverage of broader interests. It is possible to err in either direction.

10.

The Lecture

EVERYONE is familiar with the group situation in which a qualified speaker delivers a lecture, or a speech, to an audience. It is probably the most commonly used group technique — and is also probably the most over-used. This does not imply that it is inherently a poor technique, but that it is often used when another would serve the purpose better. The fact that the lecture is an easy method to arrange should not sway groups to its use if a more desirable alternative exists.

DYNAMIC CHARACTERISTICS OF THIS METHOD

1. It is an extremely formal technique; the lecture permits only one-way communication.
2. It allows for complete and detailed presentations without the distraction of interruptions.

3. It is a very rapid method of conveying information to a group.
4. Control can be rigid, since it is entirely in the hands of the speaker and chairman.
5. It is an abstract form of group interaction, and hence calls for a high degree of competence on the part of the speaker and a high level of audience cooperation.
6. Group members and group leadership can exert little control over content and approach. Irresponsible speakers may state half truths, distort facts, or make highly emotional appeals.
7. It is difficult to measure the effect of a speech on the group in any objective way.

THIS METHOD MIGHT BE CHOSEN . . .

1. To present information in a formal and direct manner.
2. To supply expert information, with continuity.
3. To identify a problem, or a general problem area.
4. To explore certain limited facets of a problem.
5. To explore one or several solutions to a problem.
6. To stimulate the group to additional reading and/or discussion.
7. To inspire the group.
8. To divert or entertain a group by use of a very skilled or very experienced speaker.
9. To help the group share the experiences of another person vicariously.

THIS METHOD IS USEFUL . . .

1. When group standards, identity, and social controls are such that group member attention and interest will be maintained in a one-way communication situation.

A speech is a group situation in which a qualified speaker delivers a prepared discourse.

2. When the group has resource people at its disposal, who have information of importance and who have the skill and desire to prepare a speech to impart such information.
3. When the group members have the abilities to deal with the more abstract one-way verbal communication.
4. When overt verbal participation is not considered essential to group member listening and learning.
5. When the more passive "listener" role is acceptable to group members.
6. When the group members wish to share vicariously in the experiences of another person.
7. When there exists a high degree of group identity with the problem and/or person making the presentation.
8. When the group is so large as to make overt total group participation difficult to attain.
9. When there is an atmosphere in which the group will accept ideas or stimulation from "outsiders."
10. When there is not time in the meeting structuring to allow for entire group or subgroup participation.
11. When there is limited group time for preparation — the chairman and speaker can organize the presentation.

HOW TO USE THIS METHOD
The Group Should:

1. Have clearly in mind the objective(s) of the meeting and the particular segment of the meeting in which this technique might be used.
2. Consider alternative means that might be used to accomplish this objective. (Remembering that the speech is one of the more over-used techniques.)
3. Inform the potential speaker of the subject it wishes presented and obtain his consent to speak on that subject.

4. Provide a situation in which group members can be physically comfortable and such seating arrangements that all members can both clearly see and hear the speaker.
5. Determine with the speaker the need for amplifying equipment, projector, and other aids.

A Good Chairman Should:

1. Decide, in consultation with group members, on the topic or problem to be presented.
2. Make sure the speaker chosen is qualified.
3. Contact the speaker as far in advance of the meeting as is possible (or appoint a committee to do so).
4. Inform the potential speaker of the topic upon which he will be expected to speak, the length of time he has, and in a general way what the group hopes to get from listening to him.
5. Inform the speaker prior to the meeting night of the size of the audience expected.
6. Inform the speaker on how his speech will fit into the over-all activities of the group.
7. See that all necessary arrangements are made for the meeting.
8. Call the meeting to order and set the general framework for the speaker.
9. Introduce the speaker to the audience as concisely as possible; give only enough background information

Determine the speaker's preferences on amplifying equipment.

to indicate his qualifications to speak on the topic, no more. Personal puffery and "pedigree reading" usually embarrasses the speaker and bores the group.

10. Thank the speaker for his contribution to the assembled members and proceed with the next part of the meeting or adjourn it if the speech is the entire content of the meeting.

A Good Speaker Will:

1. Accept a speaking engagement only if qualified and willing to prepare an organized speech.
2. Organize the lecture to fit the needs of the group as he knows it from communication with group representatives.
3. Respect the wishes of the chairman and group by keeping within allotted time.

Good Group Members Should:

1. Prepare themselves so that they may obtain as much as possible from the speaker. This may involve reading up on the subject, discussing the subject with other group members, or individual thought on the subject.
2. Come to the meeting with an open mind and willingness to listen to the points made by the speaker.
3. Listen attentively.
4. Think during and after the speech and attempt to integrate any new factual or logical ideas presented with existing ideas.
5. Extend all common courtesies to the speaker.

CAUTIONS

1. Do not over-use this method.
2. The lecture is inferior to the symposium for bringing out divergent points of view upon a subject.
3. It is inferior to the huddle or buzz groups in moving a group toward consensus or action.

4. It is inferior to the panel for bringing about a resolution of differences of opinion among a group.

5. It is inferior to an interrogator panel in getting answers to specific questions a group may want to have answered.

6. It is inferior to the interview in bringing the most interesting (to the group) unique experiences of a traveler or other person to a group. This is particularly true if some technique such as huddle or buzz is used to get interview format set up.

7. It is inferior to role playing in getting group members to see the point of view of others in a controversial situation.

8. A major defect of the speech or lecture is that it is "the easiest way out" for the chairman or others who have formal responsibility for group meetings. It is deceptively easy, for while it may be relatively easy to line up a speaker, the freedom he has and will exercise may mean that he may divert the group so that they will have difficulty getting back on the track of reaching their own goals. In many cases the speech may be interesting or informative but not really related to the specified goals of the group.

9. The technique demands a high level of ability on the part of the speakers and the audience in dealing with abstractions.

10. Unless a group definitely wishes to learn, it will respond poorly to being lectured.

TECHNIQUE

11.

Brainstorming

BRAINSTORMING is a type of small group interaction designed to encourage the free introduction of ideas on an unrestricted basis and without any limitations as to feasibility. Brainstorming makes it possible for a group to consider alternative solutions to problems unhampered by organizational, institutional, or financial restrictions, or by limitations of skills or abilities. All ideas are accepted without challenge, except as they may conflict with any ground rules previously laid down.

Brainstorming is often relatively unrestricted, but it is possible to limit it to a single problem, or to solutions for a single problem. Sometimes a brainstorming session on a broad problem area may be followed by a session on some more restricted aspect of the problem.

DYNAMIC CHARACTERISTICS OF THIS METHOD

1. It is completely informal.
2. It permits discussion of a problem without consideration of any of the usual restrictions or inhibitions.
3. It gives the group an opportunity to consider many alternatives, not just those which fall within their perceived range of abilities.
4. It provides maximum opportunity for interstimulation and creativity among members.
5. Because of the easy exchange of ideas and opinions inherent in the method it often has value in the building of group morale and esprit de corps.

THIS METHOD MIGHT BE CHOSEN . . .

1. To allow for maximum creativity and interstimulation.
2. To make a clean break from traditional objectives, means, and activities and to explore new possibilities.
3. To make possible a look at all courses of action.
4. To make certain that no aspects of a problem have been overlooked.

Brainstorming provides maximum opportunity for interstimulation and creativity among group members.

5. To set an atmosphere of thought and communication that allows for the consideration of major changes in existing group policies.
6. To secure, through the release from restrictions, new and dynamic ideas, some of which may be very useful.

THIS METHOD IS USEFUL . . .

1. When the group is composed of relatively mature individuals and when group members know each other well enough to express themselves freely.
2. When the atmosphere can be created in which complete freedom of expression is acceptable.
3. When the specific role expectation and status patterns in the group can be minimized so that the creation of ideas rather than who suggests the ideas becomes the important thing.
4. When individual group members have the degree of flexibility to create new ideas outside the usual patterns of expectations, and can let other people create ideas without challenging them on the basis of resources, tradition, logic, etc.
5. When the group is small enough or when the physical situation will allow the group to break up into smaller units. No more than 10–15 people make a suitable sized brainstorming group.
6. When there is adequate time for a rather deliberate, relaxed approach and definitive action-oriented results are not immediately needed.

HOW TO USE THIS METHOD
The Group Should:

1. Determine that the problem under consideration has alternative aspects or solutions.
2. Be aware of the specific area in which they are to think and the nature of answers which are to come forth —

objectives, alternative means, activities, promotion ideas, etc.

3. Decide how much time they have to discuss the problem.

4. Establish an informal physical setting to help relieve any inhibitions.

A Good Chairman Should:

1. Set up the technique with the group by spelling out the area of thought with which the group will cope.

2. Make sure some person has the responsibility of making a record of the ideas produced.

3. Help set up and enforce the rules of the brainstorming session, which should cover:

   a. The point that ideas are to be expressed without any concern for possible limitations to be placed on the implementation of the idea.

   b. The point that ideas are not to be challenged on any basis other than that they are unrelated to the subject under discussion. They may be expanded and elaborated but not subjected to restrictive discussion.

4. Set the time limit of the discussion.

5. Assign priorities when two or more people wish to speak at the same time, and attempt to draw out those who are not participating.

6. Strive to develop the atmosphere and frame of reference for discussion by encouraging divergent ideas.

. . . makes sure some person
has the responsibility
of making a record of
the ideas produced.

7. Take the lead in closing off the "pure brainstorming session" and move the group to a consideration of the more significant ideas obtained in the light of limitations which actually exist.

Group Members Should:

1. Drop the usual restrictions placed on idea creation.
2. Abide by the group decisions on time of discussion, topic of discussion, and rules about challenging the ideas of others.
3. Avoid any tendency to deprecate in any way the contributions of others.

CAUTIONS

1. Brainstorming is useful to get out divergence of ideas and to bring out creativity, but it slows down the process of narrowing the alternative choices.
2. It is effective when the group is relatively homogeneous.
3. Can be used most effectively when both members and the group are relatively mature and have the ability to be creative.
4. Some group members may be unable to "throw off" usual restrictions and have difficulty projecting themselves into the discussion.
5. Some group members may attempt to use the session as a situation in which to attempt to gain status by exploiting the ridiculous or humorous aspects of the subject under discussion.

12.

Role Playing

THE DRAMATIZATION of a problem or situation in the general area of human relations is called role playing. The acting out of various roles is one of the oldest forms of human communication, but the structured and contrived use of this device as a group technique introduces many new elements. Role playing is one of the most effective means known by which to communicate with and motivate a group. At the same time it is often one of the most difficult and hazardous techniques to apply.

Usually two or more persons act out a brief human relations "scene" from a hypothetical situation, performing their roles as they think a real situation would develop. An immediate and highly pertinent set of data are thus developed for the performers, observers, and total group to consider. The role players, usually from the group, may become deeply psychologically involved in their roles and this involvement is commonly transferred to the group by the vigor of the dramatization. The method should be used with great respect by most formal groups because of the difficulty in containing, or limiting this degree of personal psychological involvement.

DYNAMIC CHARACTERISTICS OF THIS METHOD

1. It creates informality.
2. It is flexible, permissive, and permits experimentation.
3. It establishes a "common experience" which can be used as a basis for discussion.
4. It encourages and provides psychological involvement of the individual and the group, thus enhancing participation.
5. It releases inhibitions, thereby creating great freedom of expression as the player presents his feelings, attitudes, and beliefs in the guise of another person.
6. It is relatively easy to plan, but calls for great skill in the actual application.

THIS METHOD MIGHT BE CHOSEN . . .

1. To provide immediate, empirical, human relations data common to the entire group which may be used for analysis and discussion.
2. To probe more deeply into a subject-problem than more conventional methods permit.
3. To secure maximum psychological involvement in and identity with a problem in order to increase participation. It usually sets a good emotional climate.
4. To focus dramatically upon a single, concrete facet of any problem.
5. To facilitate communication by "showing" rather than by "telling." A good salesman might feel much more secure in demonstrating his methods than in describing them.
6. To depersonalize a problem situation within a group.

When presented as a drama, removed from the person-alities involved, there will be greater freedom for dis-cussion.

7. To free discussion from being "leader centered" (dom-inated) and to slant it toward being "situation cen-tered" (task oriented).

8. To test postulated suggestions or solutions as a hypo-thetical case which can be made to closely resemble a real life situation.

9. To carry a group logically through a series of stages in a complex human relations problem.

10. To create a group atmosphere of experimentation and potential creativity.

11. To enable members or cliques within a group to "work off steam," thus relieving tensions and cross currents.

12. To teach understanding and skill outside of real life situations by "reality type practice." Assuming there is a "correct" way to handle human relations problems, these can be acted out in contrast to less desirable methods. Some suggestions are: how to contact new members, how to ask.for donations, how to disagree without antagonizing, and how to cope with the talka-tive member tactfully.

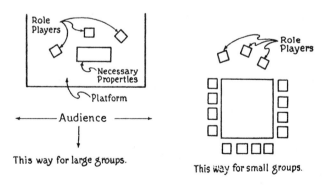

This way for large groups.

This way for small groups.

Role playing is done with a minimum of properties.

13. To dramatize alternative solutions to a problem. "Should teen-age discipline be authoritarian or relatively permissive?" After contrasting scenes have been played on such a topic, the group may discuss the pros and cons of each approach with a chance of reaching some kind of consensus as to which approach is best under the stated conditions.

14. To provide opportunity for individuals to develop insights as they place themselves in another's shoes. Discrimination might be graphically dramatized by the appearance of a group member in a role in which he is discriminated against. Reversing the real life roles of parent and teen-ager has been successfully used for this purpose.

15. To provide opportunity for individuals to "act out" their personal problems. Those who cannot recognize or verbalize their problems may gain great understanding as they present them in the more dramatic form. The member who recognizes that he often "rubs people the wrong way" may learn ways of coping with his problem as it is portrayed to the group.

THIS METHOD IS USEFUL . . .

1. When the group and its individual members demonstrate a degree of maturity which will permit them to become deeply involved psychologically and still remain relatively objective.

2. When members are reluctant to express their true feelings, attitudes, opinions, and prejudices. These frequently "come out" freely in the guise of a character being portrayed.

3. When individuals within the group recognize the need to probe deeply into their motives, basic drives, blocks, and adjustments in order to increase their effectiveness as group members.

4. When the individuals in the group, especially the role players, feel relatively secure in the group so that they are willing to "expose" themselves before the group — "expose" their feelings, attitudes, problems, frustrations, abilities, and skills.

5. When there is need to provide emotional release for group members. Many hidden frustrations and adjustments can be brought out in the open in a depersonalized manner.

6. When the heterogeneity of the group makes it difficult to focus on a common situation that is meaningful to all group members. The concrete role playing situation will provide a common experience for the group from which to start discussion.

7. When group standards and social control are such that comments and discussion will be maintained at a level that will not seriously embarrass or psychologically affect individuals.

8. When role players are available who have a relatively high level of human relations and communication skills.

9. When evaluation needs to be introduced into the group to make it more productive.

HOW TO USE THIS METHOD
The Group Should:

1. Have clearly in mind the objective of the meeting and the particular segment of the meeting in which this technique would be used.

2. Consider alternative means that might be used to accomplish this objective.

3. Recognize that role playing can vary from a definitely preplanned situation to a completely spontaneous one. It can be decided ahead of time that the discussion is going to be opened with a role playing situation or that

at a specific point in the meeting role playing will be used. On the other hand there may be no prior planning in relation to the use of role playing, but as a particular situation or problem arises role playing can be used spontaneously.

4. Recognize that role playing may vary from a relatively tightly structured device to a very loosely structured one. The situation may be precisely defined and the instructions to the role players as to the type of roles they are supposed to play may be very specific. In a more loosely structured role playing scene the general situation is defined and players create their own roles as they play the scene. All conceivable variations and combinations within the general structure of role playing may be used.

5. Decide if role playing should be used. A group sensitized to the need for using role playing might well delegate its further responsibilities to certain leaders or to a committee, but may choose to make the following decisions as a group.

6. Define the problem. It must be a problem that lends itself to role playing. It must be clear and not too complex, at least in the first few times role playing is used. It is usually at this step that there is agreement on what the role of the audience will be during and following the role playing scene.

7. Define the situation. Within the general problem context a specific human relations situation to be played must be agreed upon. For example, the problem is teen-age discipline, and the situation might be defined somewhat as follows: daughter stayed out until 2 o'clock on a 10 o'clock night; she did not call home; this is the third time she has done this; her marks are low in school; she is going with a boy of questionable character; daughter is just coming down to breakfast the following morning, etc.

8. Decide on the role players needed in the situation. In the teen-age discipline example it might be decided that there is need for a father, mother, teen-age daughter, and "kid brother."

9. Decide whether the roles to be played can be tightly structured or loosely structured. A relatively tightly structured role definition in the example might be: father, 55 years old, authoritarian, abrupt, puritanical, suspicious, "head of the house," busy — wants to get to work, etc.; mother, discipline is father's job, agrees with father, condescending, emotional, etc.; teenager, 17 years old, sleepy, independent, resents authority, "don't see what difference it makes" attitude, "all the other kids stay out" attitude, etc.; kid brother, sees opportunity to "get in the act," is a "pain" to the older sister, "keeps pot boiling."

A loosely structured role situation would simply designate the four characters and let them develop their own roles.

Obviously there can be many degrees of structuring between these two divergent examples. If role structuring is desired, it can be done by the leader, individual members of the group, the group as a whole, or by the role players chosen. If the players plan their own roles, they may either tell or not tell the group the roles they are going to play.

10. Choose the role players. Caution should be exercised if some of the roles are deprecating. It is usually better to let people who have status in the group play the deprecating roles. Care should be used in most cases to not too closely "type cast" roles. If there is a relatively low level of maturity in an individual or in the group, it may be dangerous to put a person who is relatively insecure in a role playing situation that emphasizes his insecurity. On the other hand it might be decided that the way to really make the "playboy" see himself is to force him to "bare" himself before the group.

The Director, Narrator, or Chairman Should:

1. "Set the stage" properly. Very few stage "props" are usually used — chairs and a table if need be. The situation setting depends more on verbal description than on the physical attributes of stage setting. The names of the characters may be pinned on the individuals — for example, Father, Mother, Teen-ager, and Brother.

2. Move the role players into the setting and encourage them by creating a permissive and relaxed atmosphere.

3. Allow the role players a brief time to internalize their roles. It is sometimes well to have each role player briefly state his understanding of the characteristics of the role he is to play. This helps him to work out the characterization and improves the cooperation of the group. Such "warming up" sessions should not be in the nature of a rehearsal.

4. Let the scene unfold. It should be interrupted only if the audience cannot hear, when the scene is being played out of context, or is being broken up by laughter.

5. Cut the scene. Where and when the scene should end will depend upon the purposes for which it is being used, on the development in terms of useful data provided, on the degree of emotional involvement, and upon optimum conditions of audience interest. The scene should run long enough to supply adequate data for discussion, but will seldom be permitted to run to

The setting depends more on the descriptive words of the person setting up the situation than on the physical attributes . . .

its logical conclusion. It is a common error to let the scene run too long.

6. Open discussion after the scene is played. It is often good practice to let the actors themselves react first to the scene. This gives them an opportunity to give a rationale for their actions and to protect their egos before the group as a whole comments — often a group is extremely critical of role players.

7. Extend the reaction to the entire audience. Bring all the methods of good discussion leading into play. Usually group involvement is no problem with role playing, but it may be strengthened if desired. Letting the group participate in choosing the problem, the situation, the roles, and the players helps. A specific framework for observing can be designed making use of huddles, clue sheets, etc. In any post-role playing discussion it is well to include: (a) general agreement as to what actually happened; (b) a fairly deep probing for explanations; and (c) a request for suggestions that might change or improve the process.

ADDITIONAL ROLE PLAYING ALTERNATIVES

1. Replay of a scene subsequent to discussion and incorporation of ideas and suggestions may provide much new material for a study in depth. The same players may be used, or some or all of them may be changed. It is often useful to ask the severest critic to show how he would have played the role.

2. When involved with a complex problem several scenes may be played sequentially, usually with discussion intervening.

3. Role reversals are a useful device to get at feelings and attitudes. In the example used above, it might be profitable to replay the scene with the father and daughter in reversed roles. Discussion might then begin by asking each player how it felt to be "in the other

person's shoes." Surprisingly enough, most groups contain members quite capable of projecting themselves into diametrically opposed roles.

4. A variation includes the use of a narrator, or commentator, who breaks off a scene at any time to ask for explanations or to point out significant actions.
5. Another variation provides for "asides" by the players in which they soliloquize regarding their attitudes or actions.
6. An alter ego may be provided for each player to make pertinent comments as the scene unfolds.

CAUTIONS

1. Begin role playing with relatively simple situations. It is important that the objectives are clear and the situation is well defined.
2. Role playing is a means to an end. Groups which become enamored of the technique may turn into an amateur theatrical society, playing the scenes for the enjoyment they receive rather than for a distinct task oriented purpose.
3. Spontaneity is a most important element. Structuring too tightly, writing parts, or rehearsals often spoil the effect.
4. Role playing often invades deeply into the individual's feelings and personal problems. Immature groups must be cautious in setting up a situation with regard to the depth of the anticipated emotional involvement. Skill in the extrication of a group from such an over-involvement is a most valuable tool.

The role player stops the scene and tells why he acted as he did.

13.

Recreational Activities

IN THE CONSIDERATION of group techniques attention has been given a number of well known methods which have specific uses directed at informing a group or of leading it to action toward some goal. There are many techniques which are not specifically goal-oriented and which exert their effect mainly in a roundabout or indirect fashion. These devices may nevertheless be useful, important, and pertinent to group process. Typical of these are the food and drink which are adjuncts to so many group activities. It would be unrealistic to attempt a discussion of all of these various means, so recreation has been selected to represent the large body of auxilliary techniques.

RECREATIONAL ACTIVITIES

Recreation, with specific reference to music, games, stunts, etc., is a laudable enterprise in its own right. Groups may choose to operate with their major objectives in the realm of providing recreation; many do. Groups devoted to music, to amateur theatricals, to dancing, or to some athletic pastime are prevalent. Recreation will not be considered here in this context, but in relation to its potential as a useful adjunct to the process of groups which have other definitive objectives — perhaps more serious purposes. If the major goal of a group is physical fitness, then some athletic recreation might become a major technique. At an annual picnic of a Farm Bureau group or union local, the softball game may be a very minor technique, though it could be a valuable one.

Recreational activities can increase the productivity of almost any group when properly chosen, properly timed, and properly led. Nearly everyone likes to have a "good time," and enjoying oneself in group activities may demand something more than assiduous devotion to duty. Wise group leaders try to mix in a certain portion of recreational activity with the normal procedures of the group. There are literally thousands of possibilities available and a number of books have been compiled telling when and how to use these techniques. A list is included in the bibliography. The purpose here will be to discuss some of the more general aspects of recreational methods as an adjunct to group process without expanding into the unlimited field of specific devices.

Recreational activities have great potential for developing the individual. They can help him feel more secure in the group, provide opportunity for recognition, response, and new experience. Blocks, negative adjustments such as tension and aggression, frustrations, and dissatisfactions may all be alleviated by the beneficent effect of properly chosen recreational means. They are a great aid in getting acquainted and in providing opportunity for sociability as well as bringing relief from boredom and fatigue.

From the group standpoint, games can help create a

favorable atmosphere, increase participation, facilitate communication, set group standards, and develop leadership. Restrictions due to large size, heterogeneity, and status differentials can be favorably modified. Games can exert social controls and create group solidarity and identity. Their use in reducing tensions and conflict should be apparent.

WHEN TO USE RECREATIONAL TECHNIQUES

As with any technique, it is important that the group makes sure that the purpose for which it is being used is clear. For that reason a brief expansion of informational and illustrative material is presented under a series of selected headings which classify some of these objectives.

Getting Acquainted

A newly formed group, a large and very formal group, or a group with a high membership turnover often has many members who do not know each other. A natural reserve and diffidence keeps many from initiating "getting acquainted" measures. It is important to group process for members to really know each other as people rather than as "the plump woman in the green hat." Security, response, and recognition will not come to individuals under circumstances of restraint. Communication is more difficult in regard to goals, activities, role expectations, and group standards. Identity and participation are almost impossible among strangers.

Formal introductions may suffice in some instances. Many groups ask a new member to give a brief autobiography. There are also many game-type activities which more or less force the reluctant one to come out of his shell. Wise leadership will have an armamentarium of such devices with which to break the ice and help group members become acquainted.

Mixers

Regardless of the age of a group, or of how well the members know each other, there is bound to be some grouping into cliques. Congenial members will arrive together, talk together, sit together, and leave together. Instead of a unified group we now have an aggregate of small cluster groups. Certain less attractive people always get left out entirely in such a situation. Some of the cliques will have high status, others little or none. All this breaks down communication and makes unified action very difficult. Certain individuals quickly lose security under these circumstances, though others may use attachment to a subgroup as a source of personal security. It is obviously desirable to integrate everyone into the main stream of the group's activities.

"Mixers" especially designed to break up clusters are available. Some are formal, others of a pure nonsense nature, but properly used they can contribute much to good group process.

Premeeting Involvers

A critical time in setting the atmosphere of a meeting is the interval between the arrival of the first members and the actual start of the meeting. Good leadership has something planned, possibly related to the subject problem, but more often in the nature of a recreational icebreaker. All the recreation books contain material of this kind.

Relaxers

Some members are naturally tense; others develop tensions as fatigue and boredom invade the atmosphere of even the most productive group. There is often a need to alleviate the physical, mental, and emotional strain of a meeting. Relaxing games, music, or musical games are often used to afford temporary relief from the project at hand. Large sitting-listening groups are the most in need of such relaxers and if the conditions are crowded it is well if the relaxer chosen will produce some physical activity.

Properly used, these methods have a potential for stimulating many other facets of group dynamics, communication, solidarity, and emotional release. Any well selected relaxing technique will provide some element of common experience to the members from which new feelings of identity may emerge.

Transitions

Another useful purpose to which recreation can be applied involves rapid movement from one part of a meeting to another. To shift from a general "gab session" to a more structured portion of the meeting is often difficult. At times a planned relaxing break fails to relax because the members remain too engrossed in the business at hand. The chairman's gavel which calls a meeting to order is perhaps the best known form of transitions, but everyone has seen skilled group leaders apply more subtle techniques. A riot at a football game can be quelled by playing the national anthem and on a less dramatic level there are many musical stunts to alter the immediate atmosphere. Games and stunts are also available to carry out this function.

Solidarity Builders

Many groups have no feeling of loyalty or solidarity. There may be great attachment to a subgroup or other unit, but little to the group as a whole. It has long been recognized that sharing common experiences will do more than any other factor to create the kind of identity and solidarity desired. It is often forgotten, however, that such common experiences may be just as effective if they are fun — purely recreational. Human nature varies widely; there will be some members who identify with the group only because they have a good time there, not because of the accomplishments. A wise leader gets the most from the group when he provides something for everyone.

Almost any appropriately selected game or stunt will be of value in this area. Singing has long been recognized as one of the most effective solidarity builders. Many churches have made excellent use of this technique. Soldiers march to music. Service clubs, fraternities, and many others derive a great deal of their "we-feeling" from the common experience of singing together. Simple informal ritual, stunts, etc. may also help develop solidarity.

Some groups do not consider using these techniques because they believe they do not have highly skilled leaders for these activities. However, experience suggests that groups fail to make use of this technique adequately often because they have failed to see its importance. Recognizing the need for a solidarity builder and selecting and using one appropriate to the group is important. Most groups have members with these skills or can help develop them.

Status Modifiers

Giving or taking away status is a touchy area. One of the key desires of most people is for status, but sharp variations in status may ruin the activities of a group. Sometimes it becomes necessary to "de-status" certain individuals or subgroups, and again it may be desirable to try to raise the status of others. Status differentials within the group may result in poor communication, poor identification, and much insecurity. Even marked aggressions and overt hostility may develop. Good leadership anticipates such situations and prevents them. The further they have developed the greater the problem in modifying status divergences.

If status results from activities within the group it will be accepted with much better grace than when it appears as a carry-over from some outside situation. Certain professions, such as law, medicine, and banking bring a sort of automatic status to their members as do certain records of achievement, say in politics, business, research, or almost any favorably regarded area. If this automatically given status is accompanied by excessive dignity, formality, puritanical attitude, etc., the member may be labelled a "stuffed shirt." Perhaps the "stuffed shirt" wanted to be "one of the boys" all along but was excessively inhibited. Proving the essential "humanness" of a high status individual may reduce status barriers for those who have been somewhat in awe of him. It hardly need be mentioned that great skill is needed in choosing and using these activities.

A good group leader knows his group. Persons with little status within the group often possess outstanding skills in one area or another. Arranging activities so that these people can use these skills may enhance their status and enable them to become more productive group members.

Interest Getters

Sometimes it is necessary to create interest in a subject or topic in order to involve the group seriously. Quite often

Costumed skits are often good "interest getters."

games or stunts can accomplish this better than a serious approach. Quizzes, especially if they contain an element of humor, may be an ideal way to introduce a new subject. Skits may be used to create group interest in the tasks at hand.

Tension Relievers

Occasionally there is need to relieve a disruptive tension situation. Good group activity requires a rather high degree of personal discipline. However, most people can take only so much frustration and can absorb only so much aggressive behavior without reacting in an emotional manner. Many times an alert leader can help relieve group tensions by the appropriate use of humor. Sometimes, the introduction of a recreational break into the ongoing group activity will provide an outlet for tension release.

A RECREATIONAL CHECK LIST

A few general rules for leadership in recreational activities may be used as a check list in applying them to certain situations.

1. Always have a definite objective in mind.
2. Consider alternatives carefully.
3. Know the technique; do not omit important details.
4. Be enthusiastic; create an air of expectancy.
5. Be sure all the group can see the leader.
6. If rearrangement of the group is needed this should precede the introduction.
7. Introduce and explain, clearly, logically, specifically, and enthusiastically.
8. Demonstrate if necessary, but involve everyone as rapidly as possible.
9. Play the role of encourager.

10. Enforce the rules, but do not demand a level of precision which destroys the fun.

11. Do not "boss" or encourage ridicule.

12. Stop the activity while interest is still high.

As with any method, certain cautions in its use should be observed. Briefly some of them are:

1. In the context of this discussion, recreation games, stunts, music, etc., are a means to an ends, not an end in themselves.

2. It is easy to overuse these techniques.

3. Effective use calls for considerable skill in selection, instruction and application. Repetitious use of any method may destroy its value.

4. Choice of technique should be appropriate to the group. Indian wrestling might be fine for a group

It is very important to choose the proper games in terms of individual characteristics and the dynamics of the group.

of Boy Scouts, but ridiculous at a meeting of a church board.

5. Techniques aimed at de-statusing, or at any other invasion of individual egos, must be used with extreme skill and discretion. In general such methods should never appear to be directed toward anyone, but should apply to all alike.

14.

Working With
Large Groups

GROUP TECHNIQUES have been defined as the means or procedures used by a group in attempting to reach its goals. It was suggested that a technique or combination of techniques is the vehicle that moves a group along toward its goals.

Groups often meet for the purpose of working toward several different objectives or goals. It is also customary for a group to come together for a series of meetings. In any of these situations it becomes necessary to think not of *a* technique, but rather a combination of techniques. Often this is true whether the group is large or small.

Thus far, we have been concerned with the nature and use of specific techniques. Let us now think about direct application and use of these specific techniques in the larger meetings, workshops, conferences, and institutes. The schedule of activities in most communities includes many different groups. All of them create situations in which it is appropriate to use various combinations of techniques.

The treatment of each kind of activity will be brief and only suggestive of some of the things to keep in mind in planning and conducting them. This section will briefly discuss some of these activities from the standpoint of pointing out many alternative techniques and how they might be combined in order to help a group achieve greater productivity. The discussion of the two types, large meetings and workshops, will be brief and suggestive — only a minimum to set a framework for additional thinking and reading. Entire books have been written about these techniques and should be read and understood by those planning to use such general approaches in their organizations.

LARGE MEETINGS

Think of the meetings going on in your community this week. It would be interesting to know how many man-hours are devoted to large group meetings every year. The large meeting is usually limited to one session and held in one room. This week it might be a community meeting to discuss rezoning of an area from residential to commercial. Seventy-five or perhaps several hundred or more will be present for this meeting. Next week it could be a state or national meeting of an organization with several hundred or even thousand people congregating.

Too high a percentage of one-session meetings are boring and unproductive. People leave such meetings and forget all about them — but surprisingly enough, many show up again at the next meeting. Effort to improve these meetings is an effort to increase the returns from a tremendously large investment in manpower. Any meeting so large that a high-percentage participation of the audience cannot be obtained by ordinary discussion will be considered a large meeting for the purposes of this discussion.

Are large meetings serving their purposes efficiently?

What are the weaknesses which keep large meetings from achieving the results hoped for by the planners and by those attending? Large group meetings *can* serve many functions in our communities and public life. A large meeting properly designed is one of the best ways to get people informed, committed, or recommitted to the activities of their community or organizations. Public issues and problems can often be clarified in a well-planned and well-conducted large meeting. In fact, such meetings are indispensable in public decision-making and in channeling relevant information to people.

WHO PARTICIPATES IN LARGE MEETINGS?

Two principal groups of people participate in large meetings — the audience and the platform personnel. The function of the platform personnel is to present material to the audience. The function of the audience is to receive communication from the platform and to work on the ideas or material in such a way as to accomplish the purpose of the meeting. Hence, success of a large meeting hinges upon platform and audience coordination in their efforts toward common goals. Both should understand and accept the

The large meeting you will attend this week might be a community meeting to discuss rezoning of an area from residential to commercial.

goals. Both should also understand their special responsibility and understand the methods being used in the meeting.

A third group is involved in connection with any large meeting — the planners. Their job is to think through the meeting problems very carefully before the platform personnel and the audience are involved directly. They have the responsibility for preparing the audience and the platform personnel for their particular responsibilities both before and during the actual meeting. Large group meetings succeed to the degree that the three groups — audience, planners, and platform — learn to perform their special functions and to coordinate their special jobs in the over-all design of the meeting.

Speeches, panels, forums, and symposiums are familiar methods of conducting large meetings. These are effective techniques in themselves, but they have often been poorly used or misused. Large group meetings have typically been evaluated on such non-objective criteria as the reputation or charm of the speaker, the emotional or inspirational "uplift" conveyed, or the skill displayed in platform performance. Since evaluations of these meetings are seldom made in relation to their purposes, little effort has been made to create more varied techniques for conducting them.

Some of the defects of the "typical" large meeting are: (1) audience members become passive, they listen rather than participate; (2) each individual in the audience remains an individual, not a group member, resulting in little involvement and identification and correspondingly lit-

. . . each individual in the audience remains an anonymous individual . . .

tle action; (3) audience members may identify with the speakers but fail to think about action to be taken by themselves; (4) audience members are not given an opportunity to participate, which leads to the feeling that knowledge resides on the platform and ignorance in the audience. These characteristics of large meetings are prevalent when the planners assume that their job is done when they have secured some platform talent. The purposes of a meeting are seldom met when too much attention is given to the platform and too little to audience members.

Large meetings like small meetings call for adequate objective setting, good choices of resource persons and techniques, good communication, participation, consensus, evaluation, and atmosphere. If these requirements are to be met, a variety of approaches must be used for different meeting situations. Participation by audience members in large meetings needs to become an accepted and common practice. Such participation may take the form of getting audience reaction to an issue or point of view, involving the audience in decision-making, or in getting questions framed and asked of those on the platform. Some techniques used to increase audience participation in large meetings are: buzz groups, question cards, listening teams, audience reaction teams, observing teams, role playing scenes, and subgroup meetings. Some of these have been developed in detail in previous sections of this book, and many have been described elsewhere.[1]

LISTENING TEAMS. The audience is divided into teams prior to the platform presentation. This is easily done by sectioning on the basis of rows or by marking the auditorium into right, center, and left sections. Before the presentation, each team is asked to listen for a different point, such as questions for further clarification, points of disagreement, etc. Contributions may be written down by each audience member and passed to a team chairman at the end of the presentation.

---

[1] Adult Leadership, "Improving Large Meetings," Vol. I, No. 7, December, 1952.

The team chairman can synthesize contributions and report them to the platform. Or each section may be divided into small groups who are given a few minutes after the presentation to perform this synthesis and appoint a reporter to report group findings to the total meeting during the discussion period. This method is especially applicable to very large gatherings. It requires, however, that the audience be clearly instructed before the presentation so that it understands its role.

OBSERVING TEAMS. Where a situation is being presented, a conflict dramatized, or a skill demonstrated, audience members are placed in the role of observers during the presentation. Where there are advantages to observing the presentation through several different pairs of mental glasses, the audience may be divided into a number of sections and each instructed to observe from a different viewpoint. The sectioning of the audience and the pooling and reporting of observations may be handled as in the case of listening teams.

HUDDLE GROUPS. "Huddle" groups are particularly fruitful whenever the meeting requires a very wide sampling of audience ideas and opinions. In using "huddle" groups it is essential that the audience be told of the method before the presentation and be instructed in detail about how to proceed just prior to breaking into groups. The best results are usually obtained by breaking the audience into small groups of six or eight members, either by asking people sitting near each other to move their chairs into a circle or by asking three or four people in one row to turn around and talk with the three or four people immediately behind them. One person in each group can report questions or conclusions of the group to the audience and platform. This method assures every person an opportunity to take part in the meeting.

SECTION MEETINGS BY SUBGROUPS. In meetings in which the main subject divides readily into a number of subtopics, audience members can often get a better chance to deal with those aspects which are closest to their own interests and abilities if the meeting plan allows for subgroups to form around areas of specific interest. In using this method it is useful to arrange for the subgroups in advance, indicate what they will be by pre-meeting publicity, and allow audience members to indicate which of these groups they prefer to attend. Facilities should be provided so that each subgroup can meet undisturbed by the others. Usually the sections meet together for a common kickoff at the beginning and for a sharing of section findings at the end of the meeting.

QUESTION CARDS. In meetings with smaller audiences re-actions can be obtained by distributing cards to each audience member on which he can write down questions as they occur to him during the presentation. Each question should be written on a separate card so that after the presentation the cards can be quickly sorted. This permits the platform personnel to handle the questions systematically and in logical sequence. This method has the advantage of giving the audience members a chance to get their questions down before they have forgotten them. If feasible, a variant on this method is to schedule breaks in the presentation during which audience members can write down any questions which occur to them at the time.

AUDIENCE REACTION TEAMS. When the subject matter of a presentation is particularly difficult to communicate, it is often quite helpful to the audience to select from it two or three members whose function is to make sure that platform and audience are kept in communication. The reaction team is on the lookout for points that seem unclear or confusing and has the privilege of interrupting the platform personnel so that these points can be immediately straightened out. This method, of course, requires that the reaction team be familiar with the audience and that the platform personnel be willing to be inter-rupted in the interest of clearer communication.

15.

Workshops

THE WORKSHOP METHOD has become very popular, but the name "workshop" is often misused. Meetings completely planned in advance and consisting largely of speeches have often been called workshops. To be truly a "workshop" several features should be present. The work implied and included should evolve from all the people attending. A workshop must have a planning session in which all participants are involved from the beginning. Much time should be devoted to work sessions in which all of the people work with others on problems significant to them. At the close there should always be a summarizing and evaluating session. Both planning and evaluation are focused on the work sessions, which are the backbone of a workshop. There is a minimum duration for a group to plan, work, and summarize and evaluate work sessions. The so-called one-day workshops allow too little time for work sessions if both planning and evaluation sessions are included. Two days are usually considered a minimum duration.

Workshops are more successful if held at a place removed from distractions. Sites away from the city are favored locations. Workshops held in hotels in large cities often have sporadic attendance. People too often run errands and do shopping rather than come at the beginning of a workshop and stay throughout. All workshop members are needed for planning, working, and evaluating. It is good procedure to urge people to attend the entire workshop and to discourage attendance if it is to be on a partial basis.

CONDUCTING A WORKSHOP

The steps commonly followed in conducting a workshop are as follows:

1. Someone — a group, a committee, or organization, etc. — conceives the idea and the general area to be explored, gets the idea approved or legitimized, and then advertises or diffuses the idea.
2. A chairman or committee is designated to select a site, receive reservations, obtain resource people, and make other general arrangements.
3. The chairman opens the first session and conducts a problem exploration session.

Secure a meeting place away from distraction where attendance will be free from interruptions.

4. Specific problems on which the members would like to work are listed. Work groups are then formed by the members on the basis of their choice of problems on which they wish to work.

5. Work groups meet, choose a chairman, recorder, and a representative for the planning committee, then proceed to work on the problems of the group.

6. The planning committee is organized and proceeds to plan the rest of the workshop so as to facilitate its conduct.

7. The planning committee develops a plan for the remainder of the workshop and submits their plan to the whole group for consideration and acceptance.

8. The resource people work among the groups.

9. The planning committee becomes an executive committee to carry out the accepted plan for the workshop including the summary and evaluation sessions.

10. A closing statement by someone selected by the planning committee.

WHEN PLANNING A WORKSHOP . . .

In summary, here are some things to remember when planning a workshop.

1. Do just enough preplanning to get the people there and started to work.

2. Secure a meeting place away from distractions where attendance will be free from interruptions.

3. Base the program on the problems of the people attending.

4. Avoid speeches by nonworkshop members.

5. Depend upon the interest, enthusiasm, ingenuity, and creativity of the members of the workshop for success.

6. Obtain resource people who have skill in helping others to discuss but will not talk too much themselves.

This technique of learning and problem solving is useful for either professional or lay groups. Most groups of people can learn effectively by assuming the responsibility for their own learning. The work session often provides a more purposeful medium of education than more conventional techniques, especially where every person has a worth and makes his contribution to the general program.

16.

Conferences

COUNTLESS HOURS ARE SPENT attending conferences. Many of them are held because the leaders believe it is about time to get a group together, because last year it was suggested that another conference be held, or because it is traditional to have an annual conference. Often these reasons contribute a rather shallow basis for the meeting.

The term *conference* means, "to bring together." To most of us a conference means a meeting for the purpose of information giving, decision making, problem solving, exchange of information, fact finding, problem identification, planning, or inspiration. A conference can be described as a pooling of experiences and opinions among a group of people who have special qualifications in the area, or among people who are capable of analyzing a problem from information provided by competent leaders.

Conferences are often planned by a committee that works out an agenda and then lines up the biggest name speakers that can be secured. Such conferences often begin with speeches, a series of papers, or perhaps a panel discussion. Attenders of conferences planned in this manner usually come expecting to be told what the problems are — and perhaps their solutions as well.

If a conference is to bring about group action and changes in attitudes, the delegates must be participants and not just listeners. They must participate not only in the conference but also in its planning.

Some features of good work conferences that utilize the dynamics of groups and that are based on the conceptual framework presented earlier in this book are:

1. The program is planned around the interests, needs, and problems of the participants, not those of the organizers.
2. The participants come to the conference knowing they are coming to work and not just to listen.
3. Time is taken at the opening session to review the conference objectives, the conference methods, the responsibilities of those attending, and the roles to be performed by the resource persons, group leaders, and other personnel.
4. If the conference is large, provision is made for the formation of small groups to encourage the expression of participants' ideas.
5. If the conference is large, leadership teams are selected and trained to help the conference groups achieve high productivity.
6. Time is taken as the conference goes along for the participants to look at their progress and to make suggestions for improvements.
7. The final session of the conference is used for the participants to make decisions and commitments to carry out these decisions.

17.

Institutes

IN MANY AMERICAN COMMUNITIES the institute has become a tradition. A bit more ambitious than a workshop or conference, it has served as a source of new information and new ideas for people in many fields. An institute is a series of meetings designed to convey specific instruction and information in particular areas of work. Such meetings may all be held on one day but usually are scheduled over several days, or they may extend over several weeks.

A variety of purposes or objectives can be accomplished by means of an institute. One of the most common is to present information. An institute also is appropriate to identify problems, to explore problems, to solve problems, to inspire people to action, or to create awareness and interest. Since an institute is a series of meetings, use can be made of a variety of the techniques discussed in this book.

Some that are particularly applicable are lectures, forums, panels, group discussions, symposiums, and dialogues.

Institutes, like conferences, workshops, and large one-session meetings, are often planned and conducted with a minimum of thought having been given to the various techniques that could be used. Traditionally, institutes have been a series of speeches in which the speakers, usually experts in their fields, presented their ideas. Those attending have been an audience rather than participants, and the results or accomplishments have been correspondingly below expectations.

The degree of involvement of the participants in planning an institute influences the productivity, just as it does for conferences and workshops. Whether or not an institute is a participating institute or a listening institute depends upon the choice of techniques for the separate meetings or sessions. The productivity of an institute usually varies directly with the extent to which those in attendance are involved in planning, conducting, and evaluating the institute.

. . . meetings may all be held on one day. . . .

PART

3. Evaluation

End-of-meeting questionnaires should be
easily available to all participants . . .

1.

End-of-Meeting
Comments and Suggestions

IT HAS ALREADY BEEN INDICATED (Chapter 11) that end-of-meeting evaluation is one of the simplest methods of structured evaluation involving the total group. Groups often resent and resist evaluation when they are not educated to it or accustomed to it. End-of-meeting devices are often the most effective means of introducing evaluation.

This type of evaluation can be very simple or of increasing complexity. From the general standpoint it may be pointed out that this method is only of value to the degree to which the various comments are summarized, reported upon, and discussed.

Questions are formulated and written on end-of-meeting slips to seek the reactions from all group members about selected aspects of group leadership, process, and productivity. By writing their reactions to these questions group members have the opportunity to analyze more formally what is happening in their group. Group members need not sign their slips. Once the slips are collected, it is usually a good procedure to involve some competent members in summarizing them and reporting to the group. Success with end-of-meeting evaluation is largely dependent on the discussion of the summary.

It may be more feasible for the leaders to summarize and analyze the group's comments, especially in the introductory stages of evaluation. They can then make changes in line with commonly agreed upon criticisms or recommendations. In this case the fact that the end-of-meeting evaluations are being used should certainly be communicated to the group. Nothing will kill evaluation faster than to have group members feel their comments are ignored.

Involve the entire group in evaluation discussion as soon as feasible. This process of filling out, summarizing, reporting back, and discussing should help the group identify the difficulties members feel are limiting group effectiveness and provide opportunity for both individuals and group to take steps toward improvement.

Questions for end-of-meeting slips are often designed to identify strong points as well as weaknesses. This is important for several reasons. A positive approach makes the introduction of evaluation easier and also may give the group confidence. It is important to know the strong points so that these can be maximized and not forgotten in planning for future activities. It is also important because it is possible for much learning to take place while analyzing strong points. Many times it is realized that certain things seem to work for a group but only an analysis will tell why.

It is important that the group budget time to fill out end-of-meeting slips, summarize them, report back the summary, and discuss the report. Most groups have found that while evaluation may take time in the short run, much time is saved in the long run by the increasing effectiveness of the group. In some cases the nature of the group and its activities may dictate the completion of all these steps